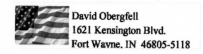

"A Country I Do Not Recognize"

THE LEGAL ASSAULT ON AMERICAN VALUES

This book is a publication
of the Hoover Institution's

**Initiative
on**
*American Individualism
and Societal Values*

---

*The Hoover Institution
gratefully acknowledges*

EARHART FOUNDATION
TAD AND DIANNE TAUBE
TAUBE FAMILY FOUNDATION

*for their generous support
of this book project.*

"A Country I Do Not Recognize"

THE LEGAL ASSAULT ON AMERICAN VALUES

EDITED BY

Robert H. Bork

HOOVER INSTITUTION PRESS
Stanford University   Stanford, California

www.hoover.org

Hoover Institution Press Publication No. 535

First printing, 2005
12   11   10   09   08   07   06   05   9   8   7   6   5   4   3   2   1

Manufactured in the United States of America

The paper used in this publication meets the minimum requirements
of the American National Standard for Information Sciences—
Permanence of Paper for Printed Library Materials, ANSI Z39.48-1992. ∞

Library of Congress Cataloging-in-Publication Data
"A country I do not recognize" : legal challenges to American values /
edited by Robert H. Bork.
       p.   cm. — (Hoover Institution Press publication series ; 535)
   Includes bibliographical references and index.
   ISBN 0-8179-4601-2 casebound (alk. paper)
   ISBN 0-8179-4602-0 paperback (alk. paper)
   1. Constitutional law—United States.   2. Political questions and judicial
power—United States.   3. Social values—United States.   4. Sociological.
jurisprudence.   5. United States. Supreme Court.   I. Bork, Robert H.
II. Series: Hoover Institution Press publication ; 535.
KF4549.C68   2005
340'.115—dc22   2005003169

Contents

Contributors

ROBERT H. BORK has served as solicitor general, acting attorney general of the United States, and United States Court of Appeals judge. He is also a distinguished fellow at the Hudson Institute and the Tad and Dianne Taube Distinguished Visiting Fellow at the Hoover Institution. He has been a partner in a major law firm and taught constitutional law at Yale Law School. Bork is author of the best-selling *The Tempting of America: The Political Seduction of the Law* and *Slouching towards Gomorrah: Modern Liberalism and American Decline.*

LEE A. CASEY has served in various capacities in the federal government including in the Office of Legal Counsel and Office of Legal Policy at the U.S. Department of Justice. He is a partner of the law firm of Baker & Hostetler in Washington, D.C., focusing on federal, environmental, constitutional, electoral, and regulatory law.

DAVID DAVENPORT is a research fellow at the Hoover Institution and is Distinguished Professor of Public Policy at Pepperdine University. He served as president of Pepperdine University from 1985 through 2000.

TERRY EASTLAND is publisher of *The Weekly Standard.* His books include *Energy in the Executive: The Case for the Strong Presidency* and *Religious Liberty in the Supreme Court: The Cases That Define the Debate over Church and State.*

LINO A. GRAGLIA has written widely in constitutional law—especially on judicial review, constitutional interpretation, race discrimination, and affirmative action—and also teaches and writes in the area of antitrust. He is the author of *Disaster by Decree: The Supreme Court Decisions on Race and the Schools* and many articles, including "Church of the Lukumi Babalu Aye: Of Animal Sacrifice and Religious Persecution" (*Georgetown Law Journal, 1996*). He has been a visiting professor at the University of Virginia School of Law and is A. Dalton Cross Professor of Law at the University of Texas.

GARY L. MCDOWELL is the Tyler Haynes Interdisciplinary Professor of Leadership Studies, Political Science, and Law at the Jepson School of Leadership Studies in the University of Richmond. Among his books is *Curbing the Courts: The Constitution and the Limits of Judicial Power.*

DAVID B. RIVKIN JR. has served in various policy and legal positions in the U.S. government, including stints in the White House Counsel's office, Office of the Vice President, and the Departments of Justice and Energy. He is a partner at the law firm of Baker & Hostetler in Washington, D.C., focusing on litigation of international, constitutional, and environmental issues. Mr. Rivkin is also a visiting fellow at the Nixon Center and a contributing editor at the *National Review* and *The National Interest* magazines. He has written widely on constitutional and international law matters, as well as on foreign and defense policy issues.

Introduction

Robert H. Bork

What has long been true has now become obtrusively apparent: There exists a fundamental contradiction between America's most basic ordinance, its constitutional law, and the values by which Americans have lived and wish to continue to live. That disjunction promises to become even more acute as the United States, along with Europe, moves toward the internationalization of law. Several things are to be observed about these developments. First, much constitutional law bears little or no relation to the Constitution. Second, the Supreme Court's departures from the Constitution are driven by "elites" against the express wishes of a majority of the public. The tendency of elite domination, moreover, is to press America ever more steadily toward the cultural left. Finally, though this book concentrates on the role of judges, who constitute the most powerful single force in producing these effects, politicians and bureaucrats bear a share of the responsibility.

Though there have been instances of judicial perversity throughout our history, nothing prepared us for the sustained radicalism of the Warren Court, its wholesale subordination of law to an egalitarian politics that, by deforming both the Constitution and statutes, reordered our politics and our society. Some of these changes were both constitutionally legitimate and beneficial;[1] most were not. Today's Court, though generally more honest in interpreting statutes, is, if anything, even bolder in rewriting the Constitution to serve a cultural agenda never even remotely contemplated by the founders. This Court strikes at the basic institutions that have undergirded the moral life of American society for almost four hundred years and of the West for millennia. As John Derbyshire put it, "We Americans are heading into a 'crisis of foundations' of our own right now. Our judicial elites, with politicians and pundits close behind, are already at work deconstructing our most fundamental institutions—marriage, the family, religion, equality under the law."[2]

Courts, even with the assistance of politicians and bureaucrats, have not, of course, accomplished this deconstruction entirely on their own. They both reflect and advance a broader cultural movement that has been growing and maturing among elites, including most members of the Supreme Court, for several decades and that erupted and became full-blown in the late 1960s and early 1970s, a period commonly called the Sixties decade. What was at first a counterculture gained traction and further radicalized attitudes among elites. The Court, now downplaying the question of economic equality in favor of "lifestyle" issues, came to embrace and then to celebrate group identity and radical personal autonomy in moral matters. The Court majority, to put the matter plainly, has been overtaken by political correctness. Traditional values are being jettisoned and self-government steadily whittled away. The American people have no vote on these transformations; efforts by

---

1. *Brown v. Board of Education*, 347 U.S. 483 (1954), ending governmental racial discrimination, is the premier example.
2. Derbyshire, "Our Crisis of Foundations," *National Review* (December 13, 2004): 37, 39.

legislatures to set limits to cultural change and to control its direction are routinely, and almost casually, thwarted.

The complaint here is not that old virtues are eroding and new values rising. Morality inevitably evolves. A society that knew only change would exist in a state of constant frenzy and would soon cease to be a society; a society whose values never altered would resemble a mausoleum. But the merits of specific changes, how far and how rapidly they should proceed, and whether any particular aspect of morality should form the basis of law, are questions of prime importance to the way we live. And these questions, according to the postulates of the American republic, are matters to be resolved primarily within families, schools, churches, and similar institutions, and only occasionally by public debate, elections, and laws that embody, however imperfectly and temporarily, the current moral consensus. What is objectionable is that, in too many instances, a natural evolution of the moral balance is blocked and a minority morality forced upon us by judicial decrees.

This judicial gnosticism was described by Justice Antonin Scalia in a dissent: "What secret knowledge, one must wonder, is breathed into lawyers when they become Justices of this Court, that enables them to discern that a practice which the text of the Constitution does not clearly proscribe, and which our people have regarded as constitutional for 200 years, is in fact unconstitutional? . . . Day by day, case by case, [the Supreme Court] is busy designing a Constitution for a country I do not recognize."[3]

Less far advanced, but no less objectionable, is the ongoing internationalization of law, including even the internationalization of American constitutional law. It may seem bizarre that the Constitution of the United States, written and ratified over two hundred years ago, should be interpreted with the guidance of today's for-

---

3. *Board of County Commissioners, Wabaunsee County, Kansas v. Umbehr*, 518 U.S. 668, 688–689 (1996).

eign court decisions and even the nonbinding resolutions of international organizations, but that does not seem at all preposterous to some of our Supreme Court justices nor to the elites to which the justices respond. The Supreme Court reporter for the *New York Times* remarked, approvingly, that "it is not surprising that the justices have begun to see themselves as participants in a worldwide constitutional conversation."[4] She might more accurately have said "a worldwide constitutional convention."

Most of us understand law to mean rules laid down by a legislature, court, or regulatory agency, acting within its delegated authority. When the lawgiver acts without legitimate authority, its "law" is to that degree bogus, but if its order cannot be effectively resisted, it is, nonetheless, for all practical purposes, law—power without legitimacy. It is a bedrock assumption of American republicanism that authority is only legitimate when its ultimate source is either the American citizenry (acting through elected and accountable representatives) or when it follows from acceptable limitations on majority rule (federal and state constitutions enforced by judges). These are contending principles and neither should encroach systematically on the other. Judges who regularly defeat democratic outcomes without any warrant in the Constitution are justified by neither principle; they have simply enlisted on the side of the intelligentsia against the general public in our culture war.

The first three chapters of this book deal with constitutional law. Lino A. Graglia provides an overview: "Rightly revered as the guarantor of our rights, the Constitution has been made, instead, the means of depriving us of our most essential right, the right of self-government. . . . The central fact as to contemporary constitutional law . . . is that it has very little to do with the Constitution." The Court has become the "ultimate law-giver on most of the basic issues of domestic social policy," and these are the "issues that determine the basic values, nature, and quality of a society." Racial

4. Linda Greenhouse, *New York Times*, July 6, 2003, Sec. 4.

and gender equality are denied by decisions favoring affirmative action and group identity while an egregiously broad scope for personal autonomy undercuts legitimate community desires for a degree of order and morality. The undercutting takes several forms: the creation of unjustified restraints on the criminal justice system that make policing, prosecution, and punishment difficult, often inordinately delayed, and sometimes impossible; disapproval of laws reinforcing morality, particularly in sexual matters, to the detriment of marriage, families, and the traditional moral order; virulent antagonism to public displays of religion; and, in a stunning inversion of the First Amendment's guarantee of freedom of speech, protection of the worst forms of pornography and vulgarity but approval of even prior restraints on political speech, historically the heart of the Amendment. Graglia's comprehensive indictment is entirely justified. The contest is one between democracy and oligarchy, and for half a century the oligarchs have been winning.

Gary L. McDowell brings into focus a major doctrine of relatively recent invention—the right of privacy—that has been used by the Court to constitutionalize the sexual revolution. Originally, as McDowell shows, the right of privacy was suggested in an article co-authored by Louis Brandeis as a tort doctrine to protect people from an intrusive press. On the Court, Brandeis tried to elevate privacy to constitutional status in a dissent extolling "the right to be let alone—the most comprehensive of rights and the right most valued by civilized men." That was surely merely empty rhetoric, for, as McDowell notes, the right is "utterly at odds with the very possibility of constitutional self-government."

The Court, in a 1965 opinion by Justice William O. Douglas, concocted a constitutional right to "privacy" in order to strike down a Connecticut law prohibiting the use of contraceptives[5]—a law that, for obvious reasons, was applied rarely and then only against birth control clinics that advertised contraceptives. The word "pri-

5. *Griswold v. Connecticut*, 381 U.S. 479 (1965).

vacy" has such favorable connotations, however, that it has proved impossible to confine it or to convince Americans that the doctrine had little to do with privacy and everything to do with freeing judges to do whatever they want. The question, Privacy to do what?, has little resonance. It was not long before the Court began to answer that question. More laws regulating sexual morality were invalidated, and the trend reached a crescendo with the 1973 invention by the Court of a right to abortion. So solicitous has the Court been in advancing abortion rights that it has even struck down laws requiring that parents be given notice when a minor child seeks an abortion, and it has refused to allow states to ban even partial-birth abortions, which are the moral equivalent of infanticide.

One might suppose that any number of Court decisions, particularly the right to abortion invented in *Roe v. Wade*,[6] would qualify as the high-water mark of judicial arrogance, but McDowell awards that distinction to the separate concurrence of Justices Sandra Day O'Connor, Anthony Kennedy, and David Souter in *Planned Parenthood of Southeastern Pennsylvania v. Casey* (1993),[7] upholding a somewhat modified abortion right. "What was most shocking" about that opinion, McDowell writes, "was the utter disdain it reflected for the idea of popular government." The concurrence said the Court has the authority to "speak before all others for [the people's] constitutional ideals," and, moreover, the people's willingness to accept what the Court tells them are their ideals is what gives "legitimacy to the people as 'a nation dedicated to the rule of law.'" Why, one might ask, must the citizens of a free republic accept what the Court tells them are their own ideals? And why is it the legitimacy of the people that is in question rather than the legitimacy of the Court? It reminds one of Bertolt Brecht's jest: the people have lost the confidence of the government and a new

6. 410 U.S. 113 (1973).
7. 505 U.S. 833 (1993).

people must be formed. McDowell, like Graglia, is not optimistic about the future: "as history shows, there is no reason to think that the expansion of . . . judicially created right[s] has reached its limits."

Terry Eastland provides a comprehensive survey of the Supreme Court's religion decisions under the First Amendment. Whereas much of modern constitutional jurisprudence, as Graglia and McDowell demonstrate, consists of rights conjured up out of thin air, Eastland shows that the Court has so deformed a real constitutional provision that it bears little discernible relation to anything the framers and ratifiers understood themselves to be saying.

Of the two religion clauses—the one forbidding an establishment of religion and the other guaranteeing its free exercise—it is the establishment clause that has suffered the most abuse. Both the text and the history of its adoption show conclusively that what was to be placed beyond Congress's power was the establishment of churches on the then-familiar European model. The anti-establishment clause manifested no hostility to organized religion as such nor any intention to forbid Congress from aiding religion generally. No amount of historical demonstration of what was intended[8] has been capable, however, of deflecting a majority of the justices from antagonism to religion. Striking down a Pennsylvania law requiring that the school day begin with a reading from the Bible and with student recitation of the Lord's Prayer, though a student could be excused on the written request of a parent, the Court said that this "breach of [constitutional] neutrality that is today a trickling stream may all too soon become a raging torrent."[9] Have the justices no knowledge of history? For a century and a half the Republic staggered along without the Court's protection

8. Philip Hamburger, *Separation of Church and State* (Cambridge, Mass.: Harvard University Press, 2002).
   9. *Abington School District v. Schempp*, 374 U.S. 203, 225 (1963).

from the perils of religion, and the trickling stream never achieved even the status of a sluggish creek. Vibrant religion there was, but no hint of theocracy or religious war. Now, under the tutelage of the Court and the American Civil Liberties Union, religious symbols and speech must everywhere be suppressed.

If any other kind of symbolism or speech, say, advocacy of Maoism, were expunged by government as thoroughly as are manifestations of religion, cries of censorship would resound throughout the land, and the Supreme Court would without doubt find the ban unconstitutional. The effect of the Court's consistent denigration of religion in the name of the Constitution must be to so marginalize religion in our public life as to weaken the influence of religion throughout the society. As Eastland remarks, "Legal scholars agree that [the Court's religion jurisprudence] is an intellectual mess. Unfortunately, that is not the worst that can be said about it. The truth is that the Court's religion decisions have done serious damage to the country." Perhaps the Court's majority is so antagonistic to religion because religion, at least its orthodox varieties, stands in the way of the moral relativism to which the Court seems dedicated.

At the outset, I made the claim that today's Court manifests one of the less attractive hangovers from the Sixties, that it is, in fact, enacting, in the name of the Constitution, the modern liberal agenda of political correctness. That, I believe, is indisputable, shown not only by the decisions of the Court discussed in the chapters by Graglia, McDowell, and Eastland but by a comparison of the rhetoric of the Court majority and that of the founding document of the Sixties New Left, the 1962 *Port Huron Statement*, a document that became the most widely circulated manifesto of the New Left.[10] The *Statement* asserted that "The goal of man and

10. The full document is reprinted in James Miller, *"Democracy Is in the Streets": From Port Huron to the Siege of Chicago* (Cambridge, Mass: Harvard University Press, 1994), 305, and is discussed in Robert H. Bork, *Slouching Towards Gomorrah:*

society should be . . . finding a meaning in life that is personally authentic," and this was to be accomplished through a (largely undefined) "politics of meaning."

Perhaps the first explicit statement of this attitude came in Justice Harry A. Blackmun's dissent, joined by three other justices, in *Bowers v. Hardwick*, arguing that there is a constitutional right to engage in homosexual sodomy. Rejecting the view that prior cases involving the right to privacy had confined that right to the protection of the family, Blackmun wrote:

> We protect those rights [associated with the family] not because they contribute, in some direct and material way, to the general public welfare, but because they form so central a part of an individual's life. "The concept of privacy embodies the moral fact that a person belongs to himself and not to others nor to society as a whole."[11]

Moral facts there may be, but that assuredly is not one of them. Blackmun was saying that the family has no value except as it contributes to the individual's gratification. Presumably, when there is a gratification deficit, individuals are morally free to shed themselves of spouse, children, and parents. On this reasoning, no-fault divorce should be a constitutional right. The second sentence sweeps even more broadly. There would seem to be no moral obligation to obey any inconvenient law and, moreover, no duty owed to colleagues, neighbors, nation, society, or anyone or anything outside one's own skin. The ultimate in psychopathology is urged on us as a constitutional right. The four-member minority did not, of course, seriously mean anything so incomprehensible, but it speaks volumes about their mood that they could utter such a sentiment, as well as about the frivolity with which they justified their

---

Modern Liberalism and American Decline (New York: Regan Books/HarperCollins, 1996), 25–31.

  11. 478 U.S. 186, 204 (1986).

position to the nation. What they did mean was that the justices would choose which obligations a person must honor and that among the least of these are laws reinforcing morality.

Blackmun's position became constitutional law when *Bowers* was overruled in *Lawrence v. Texas*.[12] In creating a right to homosexual sodomy, Justice Kennedy's opinion for a six-member majority, repeating language from a special concurrence earlier,[13] stated:

> These matters, involving the most intimate and personal choices a person may make in a lifetime [abortion, etc.], choices central to *personal dignity and autonomy*, are central to the liberty protected by the Fourteenth Amendment. *At the heart of liberty is the right to define one's own concept of existence, of meaning, of the universe, and of the mystery of human life.* [emphasis added]

That is not an argument but a Sixties oration. It has no discernible intellectual content; it does not even tell us why the right to define one's own concept of "meaning" includes a right to abortion or homosexual sodomy but not a right to incest, prostitution, embezzlement, or anything else a person might regard as central to his dignity and autonomy. Nor are we informed of how we are to know what other rights will one day emerge from some person's concept of the universe.

The chaotic mood of *Lawrence* seems equivalent to that which animated the student radicals who composed the *Port Huron Statement*. A transcendental politics, whether that dreamed at Port Huron or at the Supreme Court, cannot be satisfied by the messiness and compromises of democratic politics; nor can it be satisfied by the list of particular freedoms embodied in the Bill of Rights and the Fourteenth Amendment. Transcendence requires an over-

---

12. 156 L. Ed. 2d 508 (2003).

13. *Planned Parenthood of Southeastern Pa. v. Casey*, 505 U.S. 833, 851 (1992). The concurrence was given as an unusual joint opinion by Justices O'Connor, Kennedy, and Souter.

arching principle, which is what the "mystery passage" tried, unsuccessfully, to articulate.

That failure was inevitable. As Lord Patrick Devlin concluded, "it is not possible to set theoretical limits to the power of the State to legislate against immorality. It is not possible to settle in advance exceptions to the general rule or to define inflexibly areas of morality into which the law is in no circumstances to be allowed to enter."[14] The Court, too, finds it impossible to articulate a theoretical limit to what other branches of government may do in curbing immorality. In attempting to establish a general, comprehensive statement of limits, the "mystery passage," like Blackmun's *Bowers* dissent, necessarily goes well beyond the particularized limits on governmental power set out in the actual Constitution. That is also why the Court becomes increasingly authoritarian. Citizens and their elected representatives, displaying good sense, do not want an overarching theory of freedom and its limits and know no better than the judicial *philosophes* how to construct one. Faced with such recalcitrance, the Court resorts to insistence that the legitimacy of the people depends upon their acceptance of the Court's ukases. In the absence of a real theory, political correctness will have to do. The Court, like the New Left, may practice a politics of expression and self-absorption, but that does not mean the politics is innocuous. To the contrary, it does serious, lasting, and perhaps permanent damage to valuable institutions, socially stabilizing attitudes, and essential standards.

Perhaps a better understanding of what is taking place may be gained by combining the insights of Max Weber and Kenneth Minogue. Weber wrote:

> The intellectual seeks in various ways . . . to endow his life with
> a pervasive meaning, and thus to find unity with himself, with

14. Devlin, *The Enforcement of Morals* (London: Oxford University Press, 1987), 12–13.

his fellow men, and with the cosmos. . . . As a consequence, there is a growing demand that the world and the total pattern of life be subject to an order that is significant and meaningful.[15]

Minogue lists three variants in the intellectuals' quest for meaning. (These developed after religion ceased to provide meaning for the intelligentsia.) The first is the idea of progress, which eventually spawned a Marxist version, and then, when communism's promises proved disastrous, was incorporated into an alternative endeavor that abandoned the "quick fix of revolution" for a more gradual course of instructing the public in proper opinions. "We may call it Olympianism," he writes,

> because it is the project of an intellectual elite that believes that it enjoys superior enlightenment and that its business is to spread this benefit to those living on the lower slopes of human achievement. And just as Communism had been a political project passing itself off as the ultimate in scientific understanding, so Olympianism burrowed like a parasite into the most powerful institution of the emerging knowledge economy—the universities.[16]

Minogue does not discuss the role of courts, but his analysis fits well with what we observe of the behavior of the Supreme Court and its intellectual-class allies. They display a "formal adherence to democracy as a rejection of all forms of traditional authority, but with no commitment to taking any serious notice of what the people actually think. Olympians instruct mortals, they do not obey them."[17]

Olympians are highly suspicious of the people: "democracy is the only tolerable mode of social coordination, but until the majority of people have become enlightened, it must be constrained

---

15. Weber, *The Sociology of Religion* (Boston: Beacon Press, 1963), 124–125.
16. Minogue, "'Christophobia' and the West," *The New Criterion* 21 (June 2003): 4, 9.
17. Ibid., 10.

within a framework of rights, to which Olympian legislation is constantly adding. Without these constraints, progress would be in danger from reactionary populism appealing to prejudice."[18] As predicted, the Supreme Court, which is the Olympians' favorite legislature, is constantly inventing new rights to constrain an unenlightened majority. It is amazing to the modern lawyer that in Joseph Story's *Commentaries on the Constitution of the United States*,[19] written in 1833, the discussion of the first ten amendments, the Bill of Rights, occupies about one-fiftieth of the text. In today's casebooks, rights decisions, with the Fourteenth Amendment added, take up two-thirds to four-fifths of the pages. These provisions were not extensively litigated until well into the twentieth century. It is hardly coincidental that the explosive proliferation of rights paralleled the rise of Olympianism.

Sometimes, as in *Romer v. Evans*,[20] the Court majority is quite explicit about its distrust of the American people. The citizens of Colorado adopted an amendment to their constitution by statewide referendum providing that any law making illegal even private discrimination against homosexuals must be enacted at the state and not at municipal levels. Striking down the state amendment, the Supreme Court gave as a reason that "laws of the kind now before us raise the inevitable inference that the disadvantage imposed is born of animosity toward the class of persons affected," and that the amendment was adopted only out of a "desire to harm a politically unpopular group." The argument in *Romer* was illogical. All state and federal statutes and constitutions require groups that feel themselves adversely affected to seek relief at the state or federal level, but the Court will not, on that account, destroy all government above the local level. Given its belief in the American peo-

18. Ibid.
19. Story, *Commentaries on the Constitution of the United States* (Durham, N.C.: Carolina Academic Press, 1987).
20. 517 U.S. 620 (1996).

ple's atavistic primitivism, it is hardly surprising that the Court majority, regarding itself as free from the strictures of the Constitution, has begun a campaign to normalize homosexuality. The attribution of malice as the reason for the amendment, however, was wholly gratuitous. As Scalia remarked in dissent, "The Court has mistaken a Kulturkampf for a fit of spite." Instead, the amendment was a "modest attempt to preserve traditional sexual mores." That, apparently, was just what the majority found wrong with the law.

The Court's religion decisions rest upon the same foundation, fear of reactionary populism that will convert a trickle into a torrent. But there is something more: Olympianism, as Minogue notes, though fiercely secular, has the characteristics of a religion. That is why it is unflaggingly hostile to Christianity. "Real religions . . . don't much like each other; they are, after all, competitors. Olympianism, however, is in the interesting position of being a kind of religion which does not recognize itself as such, and indeed claims a cognitive superiority to religion in general."[21] It is impossible, I think, to read Eastland's chapter without recognizing the truth of that insight. It is probably also the case that a Court devoted to radical autonomy for individuals is hostile to religion because religion, like morals legislation, attempts to set limits to acceptable behavior. Religion and law are not merely parallel in this endeavor. Such laws (regulating abortion and prohibiting homosexual sodomy, for example) often enough flow directly from religious belief. Whether or not individual members of the Court are themselves religious, they are swayed by a false history and by the moral atmosphere of the intellectual class.

Political correctness is not confined, of course, to moral relativism. The "pc" impulse also frequently requires the submergence of individuals into groups, usually groups viewed as victimized.

___

21. Minogue, "'Christophobia' and the West," 10.

The results are constitutionally indefensible. Contrast, for example, *Grutter v. Bollinger*[22] with *United States v. Virginia*.[23] In *Grutter*, the Court approved racial preferences in admissions by the law school of the University of Michigan, despite the Court's own rule that such discrimination is subject to strict scrutiny to ensure that the discrimination is required by a "compelling interest." Justice O'Connor's opinion for the Court easily found such an interest: racial diversity. "The Law School's educational judgment that such diversity is essential to its educational mission is one to which we defer." But not an iota of deference was accorded in *Virginia* to the Virginia Military Institute's educational judgment that an all-male student body was essential to its "adversative" method of education. Yet sex discrimination is required to meet a much lower standard of justification ("intermediate scrutiny") than racial discrimination. It is difficult not to conclude that the disparate results were based on current elite moods that favor preferences for racial minorities and women but abhor preferences for white males. The latter are incompatible with "diversity" and feminism.

Grutter contained one other strand that is worth remark: the politics of group identity. Among the evils of Communism and Nazism was the attempt to reduce the individual to his group, in the first case to his class status, in the second to his racial group. Though it has taken a far milder form, something of the sort is happening in the United States with the importation into public policy in general and into constitutional law in particular of the concepts of multiculturalism and diversity. Individuals are to a degree reduced to their race, ethnic group, or sex. It is assumed, or sometimes insisted, that individuals think and behave as their group is supposed to do. Stereotyping, once considered wrong, has become a politically correct virtue. Thus the Court embraced that

22. 539 U.S. 305 (2003).
23. 518 U.S. 515 (1996).

notion in *Grutter* even while denying that stereotyping was involved. The majority disavowed any belief that an individual's thinking could be expected to reflect his membership in a racial group: "The Law School does not premise its need for critical mass [of each minority] on 'any belief that minority students always (or even consistently) express some characteristically minority view-point on any issue.'" The opinion immediately went on, however, to adopt something almost indistinguishable from what was denied: "Just as growing up in a particular region or having particular professional experiences is likely to affect an individual's views, so too is one's own, unique experience of being a racial minority in a society, like our own, in which race unfortunately still matters." *Grutter* thus not only mocks the equal protection clause of the Fourteenth Amendment and the explicit command of the 1964 Civil Rights Act but contains more than a whiff of the notion that blacks and American Indians (the favored groups) bring diversity to the classroom because their "unique experience" leads them to think as blacks and Indians.

The tendency of that notion, of course, is to inform those minorities that they are expected to display certain attitudes. Members of preferred groups are thus given rights on the premise, and the implied promise, that they will display the correct attitudes. That reinforces the stereotypes the law school claims to want to diminish. So strong has this thinking become in the elite world that blacks and women who arrive at conclusions unacceptable to the elites are often said not to be real blacks or women. Clarence Thomas and Jeane Kirkpatrick come to mind. Elite support for the position the law school and the Court took was demonstrated by the blizzard of briefs filed by universities, bar associations, major corporations, and other institutions that either believe in the politics of group identity or have been intimidated by it.

There are additional costs inflicted on the society by the Court's systematic departures from the actual Constitution. Among them are anti-intellectualism, selective nihilism, a loss of the sense of the sacred, and the destruction of taboos.

The cases discussed in this book demonstrate that a majority of the Court is willing to make decisions for which it can offer no intelligible argument. There is, therefore, a sharp decline in intellectual honesty and integrity in the law. Perhaps worse, generations of law students are taught by their professors and by the casebooks they study that constitutional law is not an intellectual discipline but a series of political impulses. What counts is who wins and who loses, which political and cultural causes prevail and which are relegated to the dustbin. It is particularly unfortunate, therefore, that most law schools require the basic constitutional law course in the first year, which inevitably colors the outlook of students throughout their legal education. The constitutional law casebooks have become for that reason corrupting influences.

In the hands of the Court, radical individualism in moral matters amounts (almost) to nihilism. If each individual defines meaning for himself, that can only mean that there is no allowable community judgment about moral truth. That conclusion is qualified by the simultaneous insistence that there are some moral truths the Court, but not an atavistic citizenry, has access to. Some academics, surveying the wreckage made of constitutional law, approvingly call it postmodern jurisprudence. Postmodernism has been defined as an uneasy alliance between nihilism and left-wing politics. The latter component is why the nihilism is selective: those who deny moral truth frequently simultaneously take uncompromising positions on their own versions of such truth, and those positions are invariably to the left of the American center.

The sense of the sacred, moreover, is reduced to a mocked and withered virtue. It is worth recalling what John Stuart Mill wrote when not in his ultralibertarian mode. Gertrude Himmelfarb calls our attention to this passage from Mill:[24]

> In all political societies which have had a durable existence, there has been some fixed point; something which men agreed in holding sacred; which it might or might not be lawful to contest in theory, but which no one could either fear or hope to see shaken in practice. . . . But when the questioning of these fundamental principles is (not an occasional disease but) the habitual condition of the body politic; . . . the state is virtually in a position of civil war; and can never long remain free from it in act or fact.

That might have been written about the culture war in America and, indeed, in the West generally, a culture war in which the judiciary is deeply involved and for which it must accept a large degree of the responsibility. Almost every value, every virtue, every symbol, and every institution that was once taken as sacred, not to be overthrown in practice, has now been overthrown or is in question. Among these are the Constitution itself (which has become a launching pad for a politically correct agenda), marriage and the family, religion, and the flag. Marriage and the family are mocked by the string of decisions protecting the vilest pornography as free speech guaranteed by the First Amendment and by the judicial drive to normalize homosexuality. Religion is denigrated and marginalized by the deformation of the establishment clause of that same amendment. Desecration of the American flag is now protected speech.[25] Some commentators dismiss the flag-burning decisions with the observation that there have since been few or no instances of desecration. The reason is probably that it is hardly worth bothering to desecrate a flag that has been reduced to a piece of cloth like any other, all by the empty rationalism of the Court.

---

24. Himmelfarb, *On Liberty and Liberalism: The Case of John Stuart Mill* (New York: Alfred A. Knopf, 1974), 46–47.
25. *Texas v. Johnson*, 491 U.S. 397 (1989); *United States v. Eichman*, 496 U.S. 310 (1990).

Only one institution is still regarded as sacred, and that, ironically, is the Supreme Court.

Our culture's abandonment of a sense of the sacred, an abandonment greatly facilitated by the Supreme Court, is a heavy loss. "Culture when it loses its sacred sense loses all sense," Leszek Kolakowski argues.

> With the disappearance of the sacred, which imposed limits to the perfection that could be attained by the profane, arises one of the most dangerous illusions of our civilization—the illusion that there are no limits to the changes that human life can undergo, that society is "in principle" an endlessly flexible thing, and that to deny this flexibility and perfectability [*sic*] is to deny man's total autonomy and thus to deny man himself. . . . Thus the bottom line, as it were, of the ideal of total liberation is the sanctioning of force and violence and thereby, finally, of despotism and the destruction of culture.[26]

Mill and Kolakowski make much the same point. Mill's argument is that the decline of the sense of the sacred inevitably loosens societal bonds such as family, patriotism, and the like, while the resultant rise in individualism leads to conflict, disorder, and, ultimately, to the dissolution of society itself. Kolakowski contends that this extreme individualism, this total liberation, made possible by the abandonment of the idea of the sacred, creates the need for coercion to replace the institutions that had held society together and thus leads to tyranny. The twentieth century saw attempts to achieve the perfectibility of man which, because that required the destruction of institutions once held sacred, led to the vilest despotisms inaugurated and maintained by violence.

The sense that there are sacred subjects in a culture is, of course, protected by taboos, and Kolakowski argues that "the most dangerous characteristic of modernity" is "the disappearance of

---

26. Kolakowski, "The Revenge of the Sacred in Secular Culture," in *Modernity on Endless Trial* (Chicago: University of Chicago Press, 1990), 63, 72.

taboos." "Various traditional human bonds which make communal life possible, and without which our existence would be regulated only by greed and fear, are not likely to survive without a taboo system, and it is perhaps better to believe in the validity of even apparently silly taboos than to let them all vanish."[27] He notes that most sexual taboos have been abandoned and that the remaining few, like hostility to incest and pedophilia, are under attack. An empty rationality plays the same role in shrinking taboos that it does in displacing the sense of the sacred. This is especially obvious in the Supreme Court's destruction of taboos about vile language. In *Cohen v. California*,[28] the Court, in an opinion by Justice John Marshall Harlan, overturned the conviction of a man for disorderly conduct because he refused to remove his jacket, worn in a courthouse, that featured the words "F. . . the Draft" (without the ellipsis). Harlan wrote that it was impossible to distinguish this from any other offensive word and, furthermore, that one man's vulgarity is another's lyric. The year after *Cohen* the Court overturned the convictions of persons for shouting "motherf. . .ing" repeatedly at a school board meeting, at police, and at a meeting in a university chapel. In short, a hitherto taboo word, even when flaunted in public, is just another word just as the American flag has been reduced to just another piece of cloth.

In a sense, all taboos are irrational just as is regarding some things as sacred. If we experience the profane often enough, it will cease to be profane; we will become accustomed to the F-word and similar words and actions—displaying pictures of the Virgin Mary festooned with dung, for example—that we now (decreasingly) regard as off-limits. Our motion pictures, television shows, popular music, and art museums have already gone far toward

---

27. Kolakowski, "Introduction: Modernity on Endless Trial," in *Modernity on Endless Trial*, 13.
    28. 403 U.S. 15 (1971).

accomplishing that. Well, what is wrong with that outcome? A lot is wrong: the brutalization of the culture, for one thing. The words and images reduce everything to the same level; no longer will there be hierarchies of taste, intellect, and discrimination. We will all exist in the monoculture of a barracks. Ideas will be reduced to grunts of approval or disapproval. Beauty will lose its ability to stir us. Authority will be dissipated so that our culture will fly apart or gradually disintegrate.

The judiciary, having drained authority from other public and private institutions, will prove unable alone to sustain a common culture. The multiplication of rights and group privileges fragments rather than unifies a culture. Since an anarchistic society would be intolerable, the remedy is likely to be comprehensive and detailed coercion by legislatures and bureaucracies, subject to judicial approval, which will be forthcoming. The result may be what Tocqueville foresaw: a society whose surface is covered "with a network of small, complicated, painstaking, uniform rules" that "does not break wills, but it softens them, bends them, and directs them" and "finally reduces each nation to being nothing more than a herd of timid and industrious animals of which the government is the shepherd." Liberationist philosophy will have produced its opposite.

There are certainly other major centrifugal forces in American society (massive immigration and multiculturalism, for instance) and many other forces attacking the sense that anything other than individual gratification is sacred or that many taboos remain in force (popular entertainment), but the judiciary plays a prominent role in attacking our foundations. It is not difficult to see—it is almost impossible not to see—in the Supreme Court's anticonstitutional rulings an attempt to remake society and thus to remake man himself. By denigrating the sacred, by abolishing taboos, by announcing the principle of man's radical autonomy, the Court has embarked on a reconfiguration of our society, on what the Court seems to imagine as a perfectibility project. There is, and will be, reason to regret it.

The battle about the place of the Court and the proper meaning of the Constitution is but one battleground, albeit a major one, in our larger cultural conflict. It is a struggle for dominance between opposing moral visions of our future. The contending forces in constitutional law have been called originalism and evolutionism. Though the terms sound abstruse, they are actually quite simple. Originalism means that the judge should interpret the Constitution according to the principles originally understood by the men who ratified it and made it law. Those principles must, of course, be applied to unforeseen circumstances. The standard example is the Fourth Amendment's prohibition of unreasonable searches and seizures. The framers and ratifiers had in mind the intrusion of a constable into a citizen's home or office. The Supreme Court has recognized that the same principle covers the government's placement of electronic devices and requires a search warrant issued by a judge. Similarly, the First Amendment's guarantee of freedom of speech has without difficulty been interpreted to prevent interference with modes of communication unknown to the ratifiers.

The evolutionist position, held by a majority of the Supreme Court as well as by those who would achieve results no legislature will enact, is that the Constitution is a "living document" that can only be understood in the light of how the Court has interpreted it over time. Though the word "evolution" evokes a favorable response (after all, it resulted in us), that position is preposterous. "A 'living' (constantly changing) constitution is in a sense no constitution at all."[29] When faced with a new question—the right to abortion or to homosexual marriage, for example—how is the Court to interpret something that has never been interpreted before?

29. Graglia, "Interpreting the Constitution: Posner on Bork," 4th Stan. L. Rev. 1019, 1030 (1992).

An evolutionist court invents rather than evolves a new right. Only an originalist judge can be politically neutral. The judge who looks outside the historic Constitution looks inside himself and nowhere else.

When all else fails, the proponents of an evolutionist, politically liberal Court take to calling judges who would follow the original understanding "outside the mainstream." The *New York Times,* Olympianism's flagship, has called Justice Scalia just that.[30] It is the standard liberal epithet for any judge who adheres to the original understanding in applying the Constitution's principles to current controversies. What the cultural left calls the "mainstream" is a polluted current that has long since overflowed its banks and is wreaking devastation on America's moral and aesthetic landscape.

The internationalization of law displays a parallel development. There are few problems when what is involved are treaties concerning such matters as fishing rights and border adjustments in which the parties agree to settle disputes by binding arbitration or by referring them to another designated tribunal. Serious difficulties arise, however, when law attempts to deal, either by treaty or by customary international law, with subjects such as aggression, war crimes, genocide, or human rights violations.[31] Given its worldwide ambitions, inspired by a false analogy to the Nuremberg Trials, law of this sort is obviously capable of interfering with American interests and values. It is, often enough, intended to do just that. Since the culture war is transnational and Olympianism is dominant across national borders, the ideological tendencies of constitutional

30. "New Leader's Injudicious Start," *New York Times,* December 10, 2004, sec. A.

31. Fred Ikle has quite properly taken me to task for concentrating almost exclusively on problems caused by courts and skimping on the blame that should attach to "lawmakers and bureaucrats installed in Washington or Brussels. They want to lord over the *hoi polloi* in the provinces: the states of the United States, the member-states of the European Union, the nations of the world." Fred Ikle, "Bad Laws Make Bad Judges," *The National Interest,* no. 75 (Spring 2004):144, 147.

law and international law are alike. Many of those intent on altering and strengthening international law are Americans who find even U.S. courts inadequate to their ambitions. International tribunals are created or proposed, which, in the international sphere as in the domestic arena, devolve power to ambitious judges. Henry Kissinger has tried to alert us to this danger: "In less than a decade, an unprecedented concept has emerged to submit international politics to judicial procedures. It has spread with extraordinary speed and has not been subject to systematic debate because of the intimidating passion of its advocates."[32] He warns against the tyranny of judges: "the dictatorship of the virtuous has often led to inquisitions and even witch hunts." There is little doubt, in today's climate, that the primary witches to be hunted are Israel and the United States. Nor is it to be supposed that antipathy to those two nations will subside in the foreseeable future. The causes of these antipathies are too complex to be explored here, but realism suggests that the United States should be very cautious about submitting itself to forms of international governance. The last two chapters of this book address aspects of the dangers inherent in law's internationalization.

The need to resist the current passion for international law when it conflicts, as it often does, with legitimate American interests is one lesson to be learned from David Davenport's chapter on the "new diplomacy." That term refers to a process in which nongovernmental organizations (NGOs), actuated by ideology, and small- and medium-sized nations ("like-minded states") attempt to make international law that binds even nations that refuse to agree. Like much in our domestic constitutional law, internationalized law and the agendas of these new and newly assertive players are almost unknown to the American public. Davenport advises that

32. Kissinger, *Does America Need a Foreign Policy?: Toward a Diplomacy for the 21st Century* (New York: Simon & Schuster, 2001), 273.

we "watch for expansions of international law in three areas: (1) treaty-based law; (2) universal jurisdiction, as part of customary international law; and (3) international organizations and global governance."

Treaty-based law is not as beneficent or harmless as it may sound. The problem is not merely the heated, moralistic rhetoric that attempts to shame governments into agreeing to treaties antithetical to their interests; it is also the new style of treaties that pursues ideological ends and, increasingly, attempts to bind even nations that refuse to sign them. The most prominent current example is the Treaty of Rome that established the International Criminal Court (ICC), a court that claims jurisdiction to try and to punish American soldiers and political leaders for actions in contravention of the treaty's highly ambiguous terms, even though the United States, among other major countries, has repudiated the treaty. Yet even when it refuses to sign, for example, the Treaty of Rome or the Kyoto Accords, the United States, as Davenport points out, is affected by the diplomatic and policy environment created that sets the agenda for what the world will discuss.

Universal jurisdiction, a form of which is claimed by the ICC, is the idea that some acts are so heinous as to be the concern of all nations, and thus the perpetrators may be tried by an international tribunal or by any nation that can lay hands on them. Such jurisdiction is claimed by its advocates to be supported by customary law (the actual practice of nations). That claim is examined in detail in the final chapter of this book by Lee A. Casey and David B. Rivkin Jr. Here, it need be noted only that customary international law is a marvelously flexible and hence an inherently dangerous concept. Though it is said to rise from the actual practice of nations, often as not what is claimed to be customary is in fact contrary to what nations actually do. Thus, when the United States mined Nicaraguan harbors to aid democratic forces fighting the Sandinista dictatorship, the International Court of Justice con-

demned the action as a violation of customary law, though there
was no possibility of a similar condemnation of the Soviet Union's
invasion and occupation of Afghanistan, or of many other aggres-
sions around the world.

These and other developments discussed by Davenport are
steps, taken one issue at a time (e.g., the ICC, the Kyoto Accords,
the treaty outlawing land mines, and the pressure to eliminate the
death penalty), toward global governance. "A current emphasis on
human security, rather than national security," Davenport notes,
"could lead to international intervention into a host of previously
domestic values," because, as he quotes Ramesh Thakur, "security
policy embraces the totality of state responsibilities for the welfare
of citizens from the cradle to the grave." Yet the American sovereign state is better able to protect our values than are international
organizations. That, on Davenport's showing, as well as recent history, seems undeniable. International activists, however, want to
control aspects of American domestic policy not only on such matters as the death penalty but on such subjects as the rights of
women and children and the possession of firearms by individuals.
As Davenport notes, "The basic stance of the globalists is that state
sovereignty is an antiquated seventeenth-century concept that will
eventually give way to the regional and international institutions
that make up the growing web of global governance."

Casey and Rivkin examine the claim that customary international law already recognizes the doctrine of universal jurisdiction.
They find that claim to be a myth that would be pernicious in
operation. Most readers of this chapter will be surprised at how
little substance there is to this widely proclaimed doctrine. There
is, for example, the generally accepted notion that piracy was punished by nations exercising universal jurisdiction because no single
nation had jurisdiction over crimes committed on the high seas.
But Casey and Rivkin demonstrate that the body of precedent necessary to support such a claim does not exist. The doctrine was

referred to, but "[a]t most, there was a largely nineteenth-century effort, principally by Great Britain but to a lesser extent by the United States, to use universal jurisdiction as a means of justifying claims to police the high seas." And only three cases exist that did not have a link to traditional bases for jurisdiction. That hardly establishes customary law on the subject.

Similarly, the attempt to use the Nuremberg Trials as precedent for universal jurisdiction founders on the fact that the International Military Tribunal never claimed to act on principles of universal jurisdiction but relied on the rights of victors to legislate for the defeated state and on the Charter that established the tribunal. The authors state that Israel's trial and execution of Adolph Eichmann may be the only instance in which universal jurisdiction was exercised but even that was "by no means a clear case," since the Israeli court, like the tribunal at Nuremberg, held that it was bound to apply statutory authority whether or not that was consistent with international law. Casey and Rivkin examine other claimed exercises of universal jurisdiction—among them, the Pinochet case, Belgium's failed attempt to give its courts such authority, and the American Alien Tort Claims Act—and argue persuasively that none of them establish a customary law of universal jurisdiction.

Should present attempts to establish universal jurisdiction succeed, the outcome would be "international anarchy," as nations adopted their own interpretations of ambiguous rules. "In fact," the authors point out, "each and every state [would be] perfectly entitled to interpret the requirements of international law in accordance with its own values, traditions, and national interests, and then to impose that interpretation on any other through the device of a criminal prosecution." As Americans have had recent occasion to notice, values, traditions, and national interests diverge sharply even among the nations of the European Union. One can only imagine how much worse differences would be if universal jurisdiction, and hence the right to interpret international law, were extended to the nations of Asia, Africa, and the Middle East. The International Criminal Court aspires to just such universality, which is but one example of why universal jurisdiction is a desperately bad idea and poses a genuine threat to American sovereignty, even to our right to interpret our own Constitution.

The recent tendency for courts of different nations to take guidance from each other's decisions evidences the internationalization of constitutional law. One result will be the homogenization of constitutional law. Since neither American nor foreign judges regard themselves as bound by the intentions of their constitutions' makers, this new transnational law will be judge-made common law. The culture war being common to Western nations, judges of those nations will cater to elite opinion. Political correctness will arrive as the new transnational constitutional law.

The chapters of this book reflect the truth that control of law is part of a larger struggle for power, the power to coerce individuals, groups, and nations to accept particular values. In both constitutional and international law, the power-seekers are predominantly on the left, and so far they have been largely successful. That is a fact that United States citizens, insofar as they cherish self-government and American values, should recognize as reason for profound concern.

—1—

Constitutional Law without the Constitution: The Supreme Court's Remaking of America

Lino A. Graglia

The President, who exercises a limited power, may err without causing great mischief in the state. Congress may decide amiss without
destroying the Union, because the electoral body in which Congress
originated may cause it to retract its decision by changing its members. But if the Supreme Court is ever composed of imprudent or bad
men, the Union may be plunged into anarchy or civil war.

—Alexis de Tocqueville, *Democracy in America*

The function of law in a society, at least a democratic society,
is to express, cultivate, and enforce the values of the society as
understood by the majority of its people. In our society today, this
function has been perverted. Much of our most basic law, largely
taken out of the hands of the people and their elected representatives by the Supreme Court, functions instead to overthrow or
undermine traditional values, customs, and practices through the
mechanism of judge-made constitutional law divorced from the

Epigraph: Alexis de Tocqueville, *Democracy in America*, p. 172 (Harvey C. Mans-
field & Delba Westhrop ed. 2000).

Constitution. Instead of serving as a guarantor of basic rights, the Constitution has been made the means of depriving us of our most essential right, the right of self-government. The system of decentralized representative self-government with separation of powers created by the Constitution has been converted by the Court into government on basic issues of domestic social policy by a tiny judicial oligarchy—by majority vote of a committee of nine lawyers, unelected and holding office for life, making policy decisions for the nation as a whole from Washington, D.C.—completely centralized, completely undemocratic, with the judiciary performing the legislative function.

The Overthrow of the Constitution by Constitutional Law

Constitutional law may be defined for most practical purposes as the product of "constitutional judicial review," the power of judges, and ultimately the justices of the Supreme Court, to declare invalid and unenforceable the laws and acts of other officials of government on the ground that they are prohibited by the Constitution. The central fact of contemporary constitutional law, however, is that it has very little to do with the Constitution. Nearly all the Supreme Court's rulings of unconstitutionality have little or no basis in, and are sometimes in direct violation of, the Constitution. Their actual basis is nothing more than the policy preferences of a majority of the Court's nine justices. The power to assert that the Constitution prohibits any policy choice of which they disapprove has enabled the justices to make themselves the final lawmakers on any public policy issue that they choose to remove from the ordinary political process and to assign for decision to themselves.

Over the past half-century the justices have chosen to make themselves the final lawmakers on most basic issues of domestic social policy in American society. These include issues literally of life and death, as in the Court's decisions on contraception, abortion, capital punishment, and assisted suicide; issues of public order, as in its decisions on criminal procedure, public demonstrations, and vagrancy control; and issues of public morality, as in its decisions on pornography and homosexuality. These are the issues that determine the basic values, nature, and quality of a society. In essence, the Court now performs in the American system of government a role similar to that performed by the Grand Council of Ayatollahs in the Iranian system: voting takes place and representatives of the people are elected as lawmakers, but the decisions they reach on basic issues of social policy are permitted to prevail only so long as they are not disallowed by the system's highest authority. The major difference is that the ayatollahs act as a conservative force, while the effect of the Supreme Court's interventions is almost always—as on every one of the issues just mentioned—to challenge, reverse, and overthrow traditional American practices and values. Another major difference is that the name and function of the chief ayatollah is openly stated and apparently well understood in Iran. In the United States the name of the single most important figure in the making of domestic social policy in the last half of the twentieth century, William J. Brennan Jr., was and is known to very few of those he effectively governed, a shameful indictment of a supposedly democratic system.

The salient characteristic of contemporary American society is a deep ideological divide along cultural and class lines, a higher degree of polarization on policy issues than at any time within memory. On one side of this "culture war" is the majority of the American people, largely committed to traditional American values, practices, and institutions. On the other side is what might be called the "knowledge" or "verbal" class or "cultural elite," consisting primarily of academics, most importantly at elite schools, and their progeny in the media, mainline churches, and generally, the verbal or literary occupations—people whose only tools and products are words. At one time the most educated and successful members of a society could be expected to be its strongest defenders. Today, however, for a variety of reasons, they—particularly academics—often see it as part of their function to maintain an adversary relationship with their society, to challenge its values and assumptions, and to lead it to the acceptance of newer and presumably better values.[1]

The justices of the Supreme Court, usually products of elite schools, especially law schools, are themselves members of this cultural class. Sharing its values and seeking its accolades, they are strongly tempted to see that its values and policy preferences prevail. Possessing nearly unlimited de facto power, though not legal authority, to advance those policy preferences by enacting them into law in the name of enforcing the Constitution, they rarely resist the temptation for long. The extraordinary result in a supposedly democratic society is a system of law based on the values and preferences of a powerful nine-person elite, enacted by as few as five of its members, contrary to the values and preferences of the majority of the American people. William F. Buckley Jr., famously and with good reason, said he would rather be governed by the first two thousand names in the Boston phone book than by the Harvard faculty.[2] Incredible as it may seem, on basic issues of social policy, we are in effect being governed by the Harvard faculty and its counterparts in other elite educational institutions through the medium of constitutional law.[3] Government by an elite

1. *See* David Brooks, *Bobos in Paradise: The New Upper Class and How They Got There* (2000).

2. *See* William F. Buckley, Jr., "Au Pair Case No Reason to Condemn Courts," *Houston Chronicle* (Nov. 8, 1997) at 36 (quoting his earlier statement).

3. *Regents of Univ. of California v. Bakke,* 438 U.S. 265 (1978), provides a particularly clear example. The use of race preferences in granting and denying admission to a state institution was upheld, despite supposed constitutional and explicit statutory (Title VI of the 1964 Civil Rights Act) prohibitions, by appending to the opinion of the Court and effectively enacting into constitutional law the race preference program devised by Harvard University. This opinion was reaffirmed and made

is precisely the form of tyranny by a minority that the Constitution—a radical experiment in self-government at the time—was meant to prevent. The American people face no greater challenge than finding the will and means of bringing this perversion of the constitutional system to an end.

The Dubious Origin of Constitutional Judicial Review

The most striking thing about judicial review, at first, is that it is not explicitly provided for in the Constitution, although it was unprecedented in English law—the source of our basic legal institutions and practices—and poses an obvious threat to representative self-government.[4] If the framers—the authors and, most important, the ratifiers of the Constitution—had decided to grant the power, one would expect to see it, like the analogous presidential veto power, not only plainly stated but limited by giving conditions for its exercise and by making clear provision for Congress to have the last word.[5] It appears that the framers mistakenly envisioned the power as involving merely the application of clear rules to disallow clear violations, something that in fact rarely occurs.

Antinationalist opponents of the Constitution (misnamed Antifederalists) foresaw that federal judges would claim the power to invalidate legislation, and pointed out the dangerous potential of this power. One, writing as "Brutus," warned that the Constitution would give judges "a power which is above the legislature, and which interest transcends any power before given to a judicial by any free government under heaven." It would make them, he presciently warned,

---

the basis of current constitutional law on the subject in *Grutter v. Bollinger*, 123 S. Ct. 232 (2003).

4. The concept may have arisen, however, because the acts of colonial legislatures operating under royal charters were subject to the review of the Privy Council in London.

5. U.S. Const. art. I, sec. 7.

independent, in the fullest sense of the word. There is no power above them, to control any of their decisions. There is no authority that can remove them, and they cannot be controlled by the laws of the legislature. In short, they are independent of the people, of the legislature, and of every power under heaven. Men placed in this situation will generally soon feel themselves independent of heaven itself.[6]

Alexander Hamilton, perhaps the least committed to democracy of the American founders and, with James Madison, one of the two most important proponents of the Constitution, responded to this criticism not by denying that the Constitution provided for judicial review but by arguing, naively or disingenuously, that it would not give judges policymaking power. The judiciary, he said, quoting Montesquieu, "is next to nothing," lacking "influence over either the sword or the purse," able to exercise "neither FORCE nor WILL but only judgment." Judicially enforced constitutionalism would serve only "to guard the Constitution and the rights of individuals from the effects of those ill humors" to which, he believed, the people are sometimes subject. It would not make judges superior to legislators, because judges would use the power only to enforce "the intention of the people" expressed in the Constitution over the contrary intention of legislators, their "agents," invalidating only laws that were in "irreconcilable variance" with the Constitution. "[T]he supposed danger of judiciary encroachments on the legislative authority" is therefore, he reassured the ratifiers, "in reality a phantom." Not only has the judiciary no control of funds or force, but Congress's power of impeachment is in itself "a complete security" against judicial usurpation of lawmaking power.[7]

Hamilton's defense of judicial review reads, unfortunately, like pure fantasy today. Rather than being "next to nothing," the judi-

---

6. Brutus, Essay XV (Mar. 20, 1788) in *The Complete Anti-Federalist* at 437 (Herbert J. Storing ed., 1981).

7. *The Federalist Papers* No. 78 (Clinton Rossiter ed., 1961).

ciary has succeeded in making itself, as a practical matter, virtually everything on issues of domestic social policy. It has all the control of force it needs in that it has long been unthinkable—though it was not to Presidents Jefferson, Jackson, Lincoln, and Franklin Roosevelt—that its decisions will not be enforced.[8] The judiciary's control of the purse is secure enough that its approval of a federal district judge's orders requiring a state to spend billions of dollars in a self-defeating attempt to increase school racial integration is automatically complied with.[9] As Jefferson concluded when he failed to remove Justice Samuel Chase, impeachment is a "farce," "not even a scarecrow."[10] The only security provided by impeachment today is the secure belief of judges that they have nothing to fear.

Laws in "irreconcilable variance" with the Constitution, it happens, are rarely, if ever, enacted. The Constitution wisely precludes very few policy choices, and even fewer that elected legislators—fully as capable as judges of reading the Constitution and at least as committed to American values—might be tempted to make. The people do not need unelected, life-tenured judges to protect them from their electorally accountable legislators; their clear and urgent need today is for protection from judges by legislators.

8. Jefferson: to "consider the judges the ultimate arbiters of all constitutional questions [is] a very dangerous doctrine indeed and one which would place us under the despotism of an oligarchy." Jackson: "The opinion of the judges has no more authority over Congress than the opinion of Congress has over the judges, and on that point the President is independent of both." Lincoln: "[I]f the policy of the government upon vital questions affecting the whole people is to be irrevocably fixed by decisions of the Supreme Court . . . the people will have ceased to be their own rulers, having to that extent practically resigned their Government into the hands of that eminent tribunal." Roosevelt: Proposed speech stating that if the Supreme Court should invalidate a certain New Deal measure, he would not "stand idly by and . . . permit the decision of the Supreme Court to be carried through to its logical inescapable conclusion." Quoted in Kathleen M. Sullivan et al., *Constitutional Law* 20–24 (15 ed., 2004).

9. *See Missouri v. Jenkins*, 515 U.S. 70 (1995).

10. Sullivan, *Constitutional Law, supra* n. 8 at 12.

Hamilton theorized judicial review; Chief Justice John Marshall, his political ally and acolyte, made it a reality in *Marbury v. Madison* in 1803 by invalidating an insignificant provision of a federal statute in an otherwise insignificant case.[11] Marshall begged the basic question by assuming, rather than showing, the source of the Court's authority to substitute its interpretation of the Constitution, finding an inconsistency with a federal law, for that of Congress and the president, who presumably found none.[12] Marshall then first misinterpreted the statute to create a constitutional question that did not exist and then misinterpreted the Constitution to find a violation that also did not exist.[13] Because the result was dismissal of the case against Madison, Jefferson's secretary of state—a case both had simply ignored—there was no occasion for Jefferson, Marshall's political enemy, to make an official response. Judicial review was born in sin and has rarely risen above the circumstances of its birth.

It's Not the Constitution, It's the Justices

Judicially enforced constitutionalism, the disallowance of policy choices favored by most people today because of contrary choices made by others in the past, is inherently undemocratic and in need of justification in a supposedly democratic society. It can be argued that constitutional limits on policy choices can advance democracy by correcting or counteracting some supposed defect in the dem-

11. 5 U.S. (1 Crunch) 137 (1803).

12. *See, e.g., Eakin v. Raub,* 12 S. & R. 330 (Pa. 1825) (dissenting opinion, Gibson J.); Alexander Bickel, *The Least Dangerous Branch* (1962).

13. Marshall read a sentence of Section 13 of the Judiciary Act of 1789, 1 Stat. 73, as adding to the original jurisdiction granted the Court by the Constitution, although the sentence does not even mention original jurisdiction. He then found that this supposed grant of additional jurisdiction was prohibited by the Constitution, although the Constitution contains no such prohibition. *See* William Van Alstyne, *A Critical Guide to Marbury v. Madison,* 1969 Duke L. J. 17; Morris Cohen, *The Faith of a Liberal,* 178–180 (1946).

ocratic political process. A "balanced budget" amendment, for example, is arguably justifiable to prevent "special interest" legislation from bringing about a higher level of total federal spending than most people want. Term limits, such as the amendment limiting the president to two terms, might similarly be justifiable if long-term officeholding is seen as giving the incumbent enough advantages to prevent fair election contests and thereby to frustrate the popular will.[14]

The standard and much more common justification for constitutionalism, the only one given by Hamilton, is not that it facilitates but that it temporarily frustrates the will of the people, although supposedly only to further it in the end. Judicially enforced constitutional limits can serve, he argued, to protect the people from the occasional "ill humors" that may cause them to adopt policy choices they will later regret.[15] Since constitutional limits can come only from the people themselves in a democracy, the argument rests on the extremely implausible proposition that the people of the past acted in a calmer time or were more knowledgeable about present day problems than are the people of today. Constitutional provisions, for example, the all-important Fourteenth Amendment, are rarely adopted in times of calm. In any event it would be difficult to find an example of a ruling of unconstitutionality actually serving this supposed long-term democratic purpose. None of those made by the Court in the last fifty years would seem to qualify. It is unlikely that a majority of the American people have with time come to be grateful to the Court for its decisions, say, prohibiting suppression of the pornography trade, removing state-supported prayer from public schools, or requiring the busing of children for school racial balance. "Ill humors"—that is, intellectual fads, such as admiration for the former Soviet Union—are more common

14. U.S. Const. Amend. XXII.
15. *Federalist, supra* n. 7.

among the cultural elite, including judges, than among ordinary people. The highly educated, George Orwell once noted, are capable of preposterous beliefs that could not occur to the common man.

To the extent that we believe in popular self-government, we should be skeptical of the value of constitutional restrictions on policy choices, favor their narrow interpretation, and adopt a strong presumption against the creation of new ones. Such restrictions make sense when a government is seen as the result of a contract between the people and their sovereign, but much less so, as Hamilton pointed out, when the people are themselves the sovereign.[16] Constitutionalism, as Jefferson and other believers in democracy have noted, can amount to the rule of the living by the dead.

It is not rule by the dead, however, that is now challenging and undermining American democracy; it is judicial activism, rule by judges who are all too much alive.[17] "Judicial activism" can most usefully be defined as rulings of unconstitutionality not clearly required by the Constitution—"clearly" because in a democracy the opinion of elected legislators should prevail over that of unelected judges in cases of doubt. Rulings upholding as constitutional the laws that the Constitution clearly prohibits are not only extremely rare (at least apart from the question of federalist limits on national power) but should, in any event, be seen as examples not of activism but of restraint, refusals by judges to overturn the policy choices made in the ordinary political process.[18] Decisions over-

16. "[B]ills of rights are, in their origin, stipulations between kings and their subjects. . . . they have no application to constitutions, professedly founded on the power of the people and executed by their immediate representatives and servants." *The Federalist Papers* No. 84, 513, *supra* n. 7.

17. As then-Harvard law professor and later Supreme Court Justice Felix Frankfurter pointed out to President Roosevelt during the New Deal constitutional crisis, supposedly "when the Supreme Court speaks it is not they who speak but the Constitution, whereas, of course, in so many vital cases it is *they* who speak and *not* the Constitution. And I verily believe this is what the country most needs to understand." Max Friedman, *Roosevelt and Frankfurter* 383 (1967).

18. The clearest example may be *Home Building and Loan Ass'n v. Blaisdell,* 290

turning activist decisions should be seen, of course, as not activist but de-activist, as undoing activism and returning policy issues to the ordinary political process.

All or almost all the Supreme Court's rulings of unconstitutionality, beginning at least with the Warren Court, are examples of judicial activism—usurpations of legislative power—in that they were not clearly, and usually not even arguably, required by, and indeed were sometimes in violation of, the Constitution. It is not the power of judicial review as such, therefore, that accounts for the dominant policymaking role the Court has assumed in our society but the Court's abuse of the power. If the Court did in fact only what it invariably claims to do—enforce the Constitution— occasions for its invalidation of policy choices made in the ordinary political process would be rare enough to make judicial review a matter of little more than academic interest. The central question, of course, is why, in a supposedly democratic society, these judicial usurpations of legislative power to impose policy choices that legislators could not impose are permitted to continue.

The Irrelevance of the Constitution to Constitutional Law

Part of the answer undoubtedly is that the proponents and beneficiaries of rule by judges, the cultural elite, have succeeded in keeping the nature and source of constitutional law mysterious and obscure. Americans have been taught almost from birth to respect judges as part of respect for the rule of law. Only judges, of all our government officials, dress in robes and issue decrees from structures resembling temples. Judges, the public understandably wants to believe, are servants of the law, protectors of citizens from

---

U.S. 398 (1934), upholding, 5–4, state debtor-relief legislation clearly prohibited by the Contracts Clause. On this rare, if not only, occasion that the Court actually encountered a clearly unconstitutional statute, it upheld it, illustrating that constitutional limits depending on judicial enforcement may prove to be no limits at all.

powerful and untrustworthy bureaucrats and other government officials. It is apparently difficult for the public to recognize the extent
to which the judges are power-wielding government officials themselves, and indeed the most dangerous because for relief from the
decrees of oppressive judges, as in the forced-busing cases, there
is no court to which one can turn.

That the Constitution has little to do with constitutional law
should be too clear to be a serious matter of controversy. The
Constitution is a very short and apparently straightforward document, easily printed with all amendments, repealers, and obsolete
matter on a dozen ordinary book pages. It is not at all like the
Bible, the Talmud, or even the Tax Code, extensive tomes in which
many things may be found with diligent search. It was adopted in
1789, replacing the short-lived Articles of Confederation, not to
provide greater protection for individual rights—a stronger national
government was rightly seen as a danger to liberty—but mainly for
pressing financial and commercial reasons. The new national government, the Constitution's proponents claimed, would be a government of limited powers, but its powers—including the power to
tax in order "to provide for the common defense and general welfare," the power to regulate interstate and foreign commerce, and
the power to make war—were stated broadly enough to make them,
as proved to be the case, very difficult to confine. Nor does it seem
that the American people really want them to be confined; federalism is highly praised in theory, but rightly or wrongly, the people
seem in practice to want a "normal" national government, one that
is, like those of other countries, capable of dealing with whatever
comes to be seen as a widespread problem.

The original Constitution placed very few restrictions on the
exercise of granted national powers and even fewer on the general
legislative authority of the states. Both were prohibited, for example, from passing ex post facto laws or bills of attainder and from

granting titles of nobility.[19] The only significant limitation on state power in constitutional litigation was the clause prohibiting any state "law impairing the Obligation of Contracts," meant to disallow debtor-relief legislation.[20] More restrictions on the exercise of federal, but not state, power were imposed by the adoption of the first ten amendments in 1791, the so-called Bill of Rights, but they are of limited scope, having mostly to do, apart from the First Amendment's guarantees of freedom of religion, speech, and the press, with criminal procedure.

Not only is the Constitution short but very little of it is even purportedly involved in most so-called constitutional cases. The great majority of such cases involve state, not federal, law, and nearly all of them purport to be based on a single constitutional provision, one sentence of the Fourteenth Amendment, which has in effect become our second Constitution, largely replacing the original. The all-important sentence provides that "[n]o State shall make or enforce any law which shall abridge the privileges or immunities of citizens of the United States; nor shall any State deprive any person of life, liberty, or property, without due process of law; nor deny to any person within its jurisdiction the equal protection of the laws."[21]

The origin and purpose of this provision are not mysterious or obscure. The "one primary purpose" of all the Civil War or Reconstruction Amendments—the Thirteenth, Fourteenth, and Fifteenth—the Court said in its first consideration of the question in the 1872 *Slaughter-House Cases*, "without which none of them would have been even suggested," was "the freedom of the slave race, the security and firm establishment of that freedom. . . ."[22] The Thirteenth Amendment abolished slavery, the Fourteenth

19. U.S. Const. art I, secs. 9, 10.
20. U.S. Const. art. I, sec. 10.
21. U.S. Const. amend. XIV, sec. 1.
22. 83 U.S. 36, 71 (1872).

granted blacks basic civil rights (to own property, make contracts, have access to courts), and the Fifteenth added a political right, the right to vote.

In the *Slaughter-House Cases*, the majority in effect read the "privileges or immunities" clause out of the Fourteenth Amendment on the ground that the way it was being interpreted by the minority and plaintiffs (white butchers challenging the regulation of slaughterhouses in New Orleans) would have made it applicable to almost any law. The result, the majority feared, would have been to make the Court "the perpetual censor" of all state laws and end the federalist system by making Congress's power to enforce the amendment (granted by its Section 5) a grant of unlimited power. The due process clause, the Court indicated, obviously imposed only a procedural, not a substantive, requirement on state law, and the Court "doubt[ed] very much" that the equal protection clause would ever be applied to anything except "discrimination against the negroes as a class."[23]

The abnegation displayed by the majority in *Slaughter-House* was not due to last. Judicial review means that the losing side of an issue in the ordinary political process has an alternative way of becoming the winning side. For lawyers representing railroads and other business interests, the Fourteenth Amendment was a cornucopia of verbal ammunition with which to induce sympathetic judges to rescue their clients from a growing array of state regulatory measures.[24] After at first protesting incredulously that the Fourteenth Amendment gave it no such power,[25] the Court finally

---

23. *Id.* at 78, 81.

24. *See* Benjamin R. Twiss, *Lawyers and the Constitution: How Laissez Faire Came to the Supreme Court* (1942).

25. *E.g., Davidson v. New Orleans*, 96 U.S. 97 (1877): "there exists some strange misconception of the scope" of the due process clause, "looked upon as a means of bringing to the test of a decision of this Court every abstract opinion of every unsuccessful litigant in a state court of the justice of a decision against him."

succumbed.[26] Because "natural law" concepts had gone out of fashion, it was necessary that constitutional decisions purport to be based on constitutional language. The due process clause and, to a lesser extent at first, the equal protection clause were seized on to meet the need.

The Court converted the due process clause from a requirement of procedural regularity—essentially, that criminal trials be in accordance with the preexisting legal procedure—to a restriction on the substance of laws, creating the oxymoronic doctrine of "substantive due process." The justices thereby effectively empowered themselves to pass on the substance of all laws and to invalidate any they considered "unreasonable." The result was to convert the clause from a legal rule to the simple transference of decision-making power, making the Court precisely the "perpetual censor" of all state and (under the due process clause of the Fifth Amendment) federal laws that the Court had resisted becoming in *Slaughter-House*. The Court later similarly converted the equal protection clause from a prohibition of racial discrimination into a prohibition of any discrimination—for example, on the basis of sex, alienage, or illegitimacy—that a majority of the justices considered "unreasonable."[27] Since nearly all laws limit liberty (restrict conduct) and discriminate (classify), the Court in effect granted itself an unlimited power of judicial review by merely citing one or both of the clauses, enabling it to invalidate almost any law on no other basis than a disagreement by a majority of justices with the policy choice involved.

From the late nineteenth century until the "constitutional revolution" of 1937 that took place under the pressure of President Roosevelt's proposed "Court-packing plan" and his appointment of

26. *See, e.g., Lochner v. New York*, 198 U.S. 45 (1905), which invalidated a law limiting the working hours of bakers.

27. *See, e.g., Craig v. Boren*, 429 U.S. 190 (1976) (sex); *Graham v. Richardson*, 403 U.S. 365 (1971) (alienage); *Levy v. Louisiana*, 391 U.S. 68 (1968) (illegitimacy).

his own justices, the Court used the doctrine of substantive due process to invalidate both state and federal business and economic regulations. Justices Hugo Black and William Douglas and other New Deal justices, more inclined to favor than oppose business and economic regulation, rightly denounced these decisions as usurpations of legislative power and vowed that the Court would never again "sit as a 'super legislature' to weigh the wisdom of legislation."[28] The Court did cease protecting business and economic interests after 1937, but its renunciation of the role of "super legislature" was short-lived.

In its famous footnote four of the *Carolene Products* case, the Court announced that its newfound restraint in business and economic matters would not extend to all matters. It would engage now in what might be called a "functional" judicial review, intervening in the political process, not necessarily because of the Constitution but because of a belief that its intervention was "needed." It would intervene now, for example, to protect "discrete and insular" minorities that it considered insufficiently protected by the political process and to improve the political process itself by correcting what it considered defects.[29] The result was a 180-degree turn away from the Court as the protector of property rights and of the economic and social status quo to the Court as the champion of egalitarianism and engine of social reform.

The Court attempted at first to distinguish its new program of active reentry into the political process from the renounced doctrine of substantive due process by showing that its current interventions were based on something in the Constitution, not merely on the justices' subjective determinations of the "reasonableness" of policy choices. To this end, it greatly increased the amount of constitutional language apparently available to it by announcing, in a

28. *Ferguson v. Skrupa*, 372 U.S. 726, 731 (1963).
29. *United States v. Carolene Products Co.*, 304 U.S. 144, n. 4 (1938).

series of decisions mostly in the 1960s, that the Fourteenth Amendment's due process clause "incorporated"—that is, made applicable to the states—most (though not all; the Court gets to choose) of the provisions of the first eight amendments.[30] First among the many reasons to reject this implausible conclusion is that so basic a change in our federalist system should not be assumed unless stated in unmistakable terms. Further, the addition or expansion of constitutional restrictions should be disfavored because they limit self-government and, much worse, because in the hands of judges they inevitably evolve from legal rules to simple transferences of policymaking power. The historical evidence is strongly against the claim that the states that ratified the Fourteenth Amendment willingly and knowingly bestowed on the Court the enormous power it now exercises over them under the rubric of the selective incorporation doctrine.[31]

The doctrine does not, in any event, legitimate the Court's rulings of unconstitutionality, because they do not in fact follow from the supposedly incorporated provisions. It is not clear, to say the least, that the First Amendment's prohibition of laws respecting an establishment of religion, for example, even if incorporated, prohibits a state from making provision for prayer in public schools or from allowing the display of the Ten Commandments in a courthouse.[32] It is even less clear, in fact surely incorrect, that the First Amendment's protection of "the freedom of speech" was meant to protect nude dancing, flag burning, and political demonstrations in an elementary school classroom.[33] To take another example, the

30. *See, e.g., Duncan v. Louisiana,* 391 U.S. 748 (1968).

31. *See, e.g.,* Charles Fairman, *Does the Fourteenth Amendment Incorporate the Bill of Rights? The Original Understanding,* 2 Stan. L. Rev. 5 (1949); Raoul Berger, *Government by Judiciary: The Transformation of the Fourteenth Amendment* (2d ed. 1997); *contra, see, e.g.,* Michael Curtis, *No State Shall Abridge: The Fourteenth Amendment and the Bill of Rights* (1985).

32. *Engel v. Vitale,* 370 U.S. 421 (1962) (prayer); *Stone v. Graham,* 449 U.S. 39 (1980) (Ten Commandments).

33. *Shad v. Mount Ephraim,* 452 U.S. 61 (1981) (nude dancing); *Texas v. Johnson,*

incorporation of the Fifth Amendment's prohibition of double jeopardy, if held to its intended meaning, would not invalidate any state law because no state permits, or has ever permitted, two complete, separate trials for a single offense.[34]

Even the selective incorporation doctrine and an expansive interpretation of the Bill of Rights provisions proved inadequate, however, to the justices' need to purport to find constitutional grounds to invalidate laws that they strongly disapproved of. *Griswold v. Connecticut*, for example, involved a challenge (in fact, the third challenge) to Connecticut's anticontraception law.[35] Connecticut was not big enough for both Yale University and a law so offensive to the Yale law faculty (a member of which argued for plaintiffs), and Connecticut proved no match for Yale in the Supreme Court. The Court, accordingly, in an opinion by Justice Douglas, a former Yale law professor, found that the law was unconstitutional but had some difficulty in stating the ground.

Having renounced and reviled substantive due process for so many years, Douglas could hardly simply declare the law invalid because it was "unreasonable," and he explicitly declined to do so. The Court would no longer, he reiterated, "sit as a super-legislature to determine the wisdom, need and propriety of laws that touch economic problems, business affairs, or social conditions"; it would now only enforce actual constitutional rights. The inconvenient fact that there was no relevant constitutional right Douglas overcame by imagining and enacting a new one, the right of "privacy." Although this right could not be found in the Bill of Rights itself, it could be found, Douglas explained, in the "penumbras, formed

---

491 U.S. 397 (flag burning); *Tinker v. Des Moines Ind. Community School District*, 393 U.S. 503 (1969) (demonstration).

34. *See Palko v. Connecticut*, 302 U.S. 319 (1937) (upholding retrial after successful state appeal); *overruled* in *Benton v. Maryland*, 395 U.S. 784 (1969).

35. 381 U.S. 479 (1965). Earlier attacks on the law were rejected in *Tileston v. Ullman*, 318 U.S. 44 (1943), and *Poe v. Ullman*, 367 U.S. 497 (1961).

by emanations" from Bill of Rights provisions.[36] How this juvenile maneuver conceals better than the doctrine of substantive due process the fact that the Court is acting as a superlegislature is not apparent, except perhaps to the justices who joined the opinion. What the alleged right of privacy had to do, in any event, with a law prohibiting the public operation of a birth control clinic, the issue in the case, is also unclear.

Another way by which the Court purported to avoid the dreaded doctrine of substantive due process and acting as a super-legislature was by finding surprising new meanings in the equal protection clause. In *Levy v. Louisiana*, for example, it took the Court less than four pages of the United States Reports to overturn the centuries-old distinction in Anglo-American law, European civil law, and probably the law of all developed societies, between legitimate and illegitimate birth. Illustrating his typical contempt for traditional values and popular opinion as well as the Constitution, Justice Douglas, writing for the Court, found support for this revolutionary decision in a speech by Edmund the Bastard in Shakespeare's *King Lear*.[37] It would be difficult to imagine a distinction that the Fourteenth Amendment was less meant to prohibit, but that is irrelevant to justices who see no need to look outside themselves for wisdom or authority.

Illegitimates, Justice Douglas considered it sufficient to point out, were not responsible for their legal status, something, he apparently thought, his less perceptive or benevolent predecessors in the history of western civilization had failed to realize. That removing or lessening the social stigma previously attached to illegitimacy is responsible for its subsequent explosion we cannot be certain, but

---

36. *Id.* at 482, 484.

37. 391 U.S. 68 (1968). "We can say with Shakespeare: 'Why bastard, wherefore base? When my dimensions are as well compact, My mind as generous, and my shape as true, As honest madam's issue? Why brand they us With base? with baseness? bastardy? base, base?" *Id.* at 72, n. 6.

it cannot have helped. It also served to make clear that nothing is so universally accepted and fundamental a part of American (or Western) civilization that it cannot be obliterated by a Supreme Court decree.

Griswold and *Levy* exemplify Supreme Court decision making on matters of fundamental social importance on no basis other than the justices' arrogant confidence in the rightness of their policy preferences and willingness to impose them on their fellow citizens. Because this constitutes an obvious abuse of office, convention requires that they make a pro forma attempt to show that the decision follows from the Constitution. This impossible task requires the permissibility of standards of reasoning in Supreme Court opinions that would not be acceptable in a discipline that aspired to the level of intellectual respectability of astrology. The justices, we are apparently expected to understand, are after all only lawyers, professionally permitted the unembarrassed assertion of whatever is needed to reach a desired result. The misstatements of fact and defects of logic, almost inevitable in Supreme Court opinions explaining rulings of unconstitutionality, do not make the rulings—any more than does the absence of a constitutional basis—less authoritative. "We are not final," Justice Robert Jackson famously pointed out, "because we are infallible, but we are infallible because we are final."[38] The Court is not supreme only in name.

Griswold's ludicrous but widely lauded invalidation of Connecticut's anticontraception law emboldened the Court to go on to the next step of invalidating anti-abortion laws as well. In *Roe v. Wade*, these laws were also found to violate the right of privacy announced in *Griswold*, but the right was now said to be based not on any constitutional penumbra—once was apparently enough for that joke—but on a frank revival of substantive due process.[39] An

38. *Brown v. Allen*, 344 U.S. 443, 540 (1953) (concurring opinion).
39. 410 U.S. 113, 153 (1973).

unlimited power to invalidate laws as "unreasonable" (i.e., as contrary to a majority of the justices' policy preferences) was clearly a very bad thing, the justices and constitutional scholars had only shortly before agreed, but that was when in the hands of conservative justices the power was used as a brake on social change. In the hands of liberal justices, it became, they now also agreed, an indispensable means of achieving social reforms achievable in no other way. It was not the Court's acting as a superlegislature that was objectionable, after all, but its legislating policies and preserving values that today's justices and scholars do not share.

It is not possible to criticize the Court's explanation of the constitutional basis of *Roe*, because there is no explanation, only assertion. Surely no one believes that abortion became a constitutional right in 1973 because the Court discovered in the then-105-year-old due process clause of the Fourteenth Amendment something no one had noticed before. But it was no longer necessary that anyone believe this. The Court now felt confident enough of its policymaking status to abandon—except for a pro forma mention of the "Fourteenth Amendment's concept of personal liberty"—any pretense that its rulings of unconstitutionality necessarily had any constitutional basis.[40]

Roe is widely condemned as the clearest example of judicial activism since the infamous *Dred Scott v. Sandford* decision that returned plaintiff Scott to slavery,[41] but it is not less legitimate than most or all of the Court's other rulings of unconstitutionality, which are equally without constitutional basis. *Roe* is important because by effectively disallowing all state laws protecting the unborn, it is seen by many, probably most, Americans as imposing a sentence of death on millions of human beings and, at the same time, by the cultural elite as a crucial egalitarian social advance. It is an

40. *Roe v. Wade*, 410 U.S. 113 at 158.
41. 60 U.S. 393 (1856).

impressive display of the Court's power—though not necessarily more so than its redistricting, busing, criminal procedure, pornography, and many other decisions—to fundamentally remake American society on no other basis than the commitment by a majority of the justices to an elite minority view. What is most revealing about the Court's position in our political system is the utter futility of all attempts by the ordinary political system to respond. The election and reelection of a president strongly opposed to unlimited abortion, his appointment of Supreme Court justices, and a stream of state laws and proposals seeking some small protection for the unborn have all proved insufficient not only to significantly limit the Court-created abortion right but even to dissuade the Court from extending it.[42]

That the irrelevance of the Constitution to the Court's abortion decisions is in no way unique can be seen in almost any of the Court's interventions in the political process. Consider, for example, that there was a time when the assignment of children to public schools on the basis of race was constitutionally permissible, a time when it was constitutionally prohibited, and a time, the present, when it is sometimes constitutionally required.[43] That covers all the possibilities, yet in all that time, the Constitution was not amended in any relevant respect. An impartial observer would have no trouble concluding that the Constitution is not the operative variable.

That the Constitution was not necessarily the basis of even the great *Brown* decision can be shown with a conclusiveness approaching that of a scientific experiment. School racial segregation by law was held unconstitutional in *Brown*, as everyone

42. *See, e.g., Stenberg v. Carhart*, 530 U.S. 914 (2000) (rejecting an effort by Congress and the president to obtain the Court's permission for a restriction on at least so-called partial-birth abortions).

43. *Plessy v. Ferguson*, 163 U.S. 537 (1896) (permitted); *Brown v. Board of Educ.*, 347 U.S. 483 (1954) (prohibited); *Swann v. Charlotte-Mecklenburg Bd. of Educ.*, 402 U.S. 1 (1971) (required).

knows or at least believes, because it was found to be prohibited
by the equal protection clause of the Fourteenth Amendment. What
if it were possible to test that hypothesis scientifically by a controlled experiment, rerunning the *Brown* case without the equal
protection clause? If the hypothesis is that chemical X causes a
complex solution to turn blue, it can be tested by compounding the
solution without chemical X, and disproved if the solution still
turns blue. Such experiments can rarely be conducted in social
science and law. But as if to advance the cause of science, one was
in effect conducted on the school racial segregation issue.

On the day the Court decided *Brown*, it also decided the constitutionality of school racial segregation required by federal law
in the District of Columbia, where the equal protection clause,
applicable only to the states, was not available. What difference in
result did this make? Why, none at all. School segregation was also
unconstitutional in the District of Columbia, but now because it
was found to be prohibited by the due process clause of the Fifth
Amendment, which does apply to the federal government.[44] That
the Fifth Amendment was adopted in 1791 as part of a Constitution
recognizing and protecting slavery has no relevance, of course, to
the role it can be made to play in the Supreme Court's constitutional law ruse. The solution still turned blue!

Consider, finally, the Court's decisions holding unconstitutional, because prohibited by the First Amendment as "incorporated" in the Fourteenth, state-sponsored prayer in public schools,
state assistance to religious schools, and the display of religious
symbols on public property.[45] These decisions are in a sense even
less legitimate than, say, *Griswold, Levy,* or *Roe.* The purpose of
the religion clauses of the First Amendment was to preclude federal
interference in matters of religion, leaving them exclusively to the

44. *Bolling v. Sharpe,* 347 U.S. 497 (1954).
45. *E.g., Engel v. Vitale,* 370 U.S. 421 (1962) (prayer); *Lemon v. Kurtzman,* 403
U.S. 602 (1971) (assistance); *Allegheny County v. American Civil Liberties Union,*
492 U.S. 573 (1989) (display).

states.[46] While *Griswold, Levy,* and *Roe* are based on nothing in the Constitution, the Court's religion decisions are actually in violation of the very provisions on which they purport to be based. Similarly, the fact that the Constitution explicitly recognizes capital punishment in several places did not prevent Justices William J. Brennan Jr., Thurgood Marshall, and Harry Blackmun from insisting that it is constitutionally prohibited.[47]

Constitutional law without the Constitution—policymaking for the nation as a whole by majority vote of a committee of nine electorally unaccountable lawyers—is the antithesis of the constitutional system, whose basic principles are representative self-government, federalism, and separation of powers. We should return to the constitutional system not only because it is the one we are supposedly living under, but more important, because it is still the best system of government ever devised, the basis of our extraordinary success as a nation. But why, then, is our present inconsistent and indefensible system permitted to continue and how, most important, can the constitutional system be reinstituted?

Judicial Review: From Conservative Force to Engine of Social Change

That allowing judges to have the final say on any issue of public policy they choose is not an improvement on the constitutional scheme can be seen not only on the basis of theory and principle, but also of experience. The Court's first significant exercise of the power of judicial review, fifty-three years after *Marbury,* to invalidate a federal statute was its 1856 decision in *Dred Scott v. Sand-*

---

46. *See, e.g.,* Steven D. Smith, *Foreordained Failure: The Quest for a Constitutional Principle of Religious Freedom* (1995).

47. *Gregg v. Georgia,* 428 U.S. 153 (1976) (dissenting opinions of Brennan and Marshall, JJ.); *Collins v. Collins,* 510 U.S. 1141 (1994) (dissenting opinion of Blackmun, J.).

ford, invalidating, on no discernible constitutional basis, Congress's attempt to settle the slavery question with the Missouri Compromise.[48] The result was to leave it for settlement by the Civil War. That experience alone, the possibly otherwise avoidable deaths of over six hundred thousand American men, should have been enough to make clear almost from the beginning that judicial review was, as Tocqueville presciently warned, a very dangerous innovation.[49]

The Court's most significant next use of the power was its invalidation of the 1875 Civil Rights Act's prohibition of racial segregation in public accommodations.[50] The result was to give us segregation for an additional eighty-nine years, until it was prohibited again by Congress in the 1964 Civil Rights Act. The most significant uses of the power in the first half of the twentieth century were to invalidate two federal anti–child labor laws and to bring to a temporary halt President Franklin Roosevelt's New Deal.[51] As to the states, it was used mainly at first to protect municipal bond holders under the contracts clause and, later, to disallow various business and economic regulations under the doctrine of substantive due process.

Hamilton and Marshall, assuming that Supreme Court justices would always be successful, conservative, property-holding lawyers like themselves, undoubtedly thought that judicial review could be a useful restraining force in a democracy. As solid conservatives they most likely believed, along with their contemporary, Edmund Burke, that an inherent danger of popular government is a tendency to make basic social changes too rapidly, rather than

48. 60 U.S. 393 (1856).
49. *Supra*, p. 1.
50. Civil Rights Cases, 109 U.S. 3 (1883).
51. *Hammer v. Dagenhart*, 247 U.S. 251 (1918); *Bailey v. Drexel Furniture Co.* (Child Labor Tax Case), 259 U.S. 20 (1922). *See Schecter Poultry Corp. v. United States*, 295 U.S. 495 (1935); *United States v. Butler*, 297 U.S. 1 (1936).

too slowly, to enact too many laws, rather than too few. An inherently conservative institution capable only of invalidating laws might provide a safety valve or brake on the radical experiment in democracy contemplated by the Constitution. As plausible as the idea may seem in theory, it is almost surely mistaken, as the *Dred Scott* decision quickly demonstrated, because power in the hands of government officials remote from popular control is much more likely to be a source of, rather than a correction for, governmental error—that, at least, is the theory of democracy.

Although the history of judicial review would seem to demonstrate its harmfulness, its proponents contend that judicial review has, like the practice of medicine, recently so much improved that it no longer does more harm than good. Whether or not it has improved, it certainly has radically changed. Largely because of the Court's 1954 decision in *Brown v. Board of Education*, the pivotal event in constitutional law in the twentieth century, it now performs a very different function in American government.[52] As important as *Brown* was for what it held, prohibiting school racial segregation and, it soon appeared, all official racial discrimination, it was even more important for its effect on the understanding of the country—and most important, on the judges themselves—of the judges' role in our system of government. Its eventual success, when it was in effect ratified and expanded by the great 1964 Civil Rights Act, made it the basis of modern constitutional law, with a Court of vastly enhanced power and prestige.

The obvious political, social, and moral rightness of prohibiting racial oppression seemed to demonstrate for many the superiority of policymaking by the Court, supposedly on the basis of principle, even if not necessarily constitutional principle, to policymaking through the often-stymied ordinary political process. If the Court could do so great and good a thing as *Brown*, what other great

52. 347 U.S. 397 (1954).

things could it not do, and if it could, why shouldn't it? The near-universal acclaim bestowed on *Brown* converted the Court from a defender of the status quo and a brake on social change into the nation's primary initiator and accelerator of social change. To question judicial policymaking after *Brown* was to be met with the response, "So you disagree with *Brown*?" As it is not politically, socially, or academically permissible to disagree with *Brown*, the desirability of leaving basic issues of social policy to the justices rather than electorally accountable legislators seemed to be put beyond question.

Although Hamilton and Marshall no doubt thought that the justices would always be conservative defenders of traditional values and mores, it has happened in modern times—largely because of the rise and influence of left-liberal academia—that persons can be and are appointed Supreme Court justices who are or turn out to be far from conservative. They can be, on the contrary, like Justices Douglas and Brennan, on the far left-liberal end of the American political spectrum. When Arthur Goldberg was added to the Court to join them and Chief Justice Earl Warren and Justice Black in 1962, the result was a solid liberal-activist majority in a position to remake America and eager to undertake the task. The Court became so firmly established and recognized as an engine of liberal social change that not even ten consecutive appointments to the Court—beginning with President Nixon's appointment of Chief Justice Warren Earl Burger in 1968—by Republican presidents supposedly committed to "strict construction" of the Constitution have been sufficient to alter its course.

The second defining characteristic of the constitutional law of the past half-century—besides the irrelevance of the Constitution—is that it has served almost uniformly to move social policy choices to the left. One could illustrate this by noting, with only slight exaggeration, that the American Civil Liberties Union, avatar of left-liberalism, nemesis of traditional American values, and paradigmatic constitutional litigator of our time, never loses in the Supreme Court, even though it does not always win. It either obtains from the Court a policy decision, such as the prohibition of state-sponsored prayer in public schools, that it could obtain in no other way because opposed by a majority of the American people, or it is simply left where it was to try again on another day. The opponents of Connecticut's anticontraception law, for example, finally got the Supreme Court to invalidate it in *Griswold* only on their third try.[53]

The effect of the Court's interventions in the political process since the Warren Court has been overwhelmingly to undermine or overthrow traditional American beliefs and practices on basic issues of domestic social policy. Some of the more revolutionary changes include creating the virtual right of abortion on demand and abolishing capital punishment for a number of years and then permitting it only with so many and accumulating restrictions and conditions as to make efforts to preserve it seem almost not worthwhile. Jurors in capital cases must be given both ample discretion and not too much discretion, making it very difficult for the states and federal government to get it just right.[54] The Court has prohibited state-sponsored prayer in the public schools, while also prohibiting most forms of government aid to religious schools and the display of religious symbols on public property.[55] It has created and imposed on the states and the federal government a system of criminal procedure, with *Miranda* rights, exclusionary rules, innumerable appeals, and other impediments to law enforcement, known to no other system of law.[56] The result is seemingly inter-

53. *Supra*, n. 35.

54. *See Furman v. Georgia*, 408 U.S. 238 (1972) (too much discretion); *Lockett v. Ohio*, 438 U.S. 586 (1978) (not enough discretion).

55. *Supra*, n. 31. *Lemon v. Kurtzman*, 403 U.S. 602 (1971) (government aid).

56. *See, e.g., Miranda v. Arizona*, 384 U.S. 436 (1966) (exclusion of testimony given without required warnings); *Mapp v. Ohio*, 367 U.S. 643 (1961) (exclusion of "improperly" obtained evidence). As early as 1953, Justice Jackson noted that the Court "has sanctioned progressive trivialization of the writ [of habeas corpus] until

minable trials and retrials in which the question of guilt or innocence is often the least relevant consideration. In this country it often takes longer to select a jury than it takes in other countries to complete a criminal trial.

Because "the freedom of speech" is a phrase of very uncertain content—it cannot mean what it says—the First Amendment is capable of unlimited expansion and ever greater reach. It has proved to be one of the Court's most potent weapons, second only to the due process and equal protection clauses, in pursuit of the justices' and academia's vision of a remade American society. It severely limits, for example, the ability of the states and the federal government to restrict the publication and distribution of pornography, including child pornography, while protecting nude dancing and public displays of vulgarity.[57] Historic champerty and maintenance laws, meant to protect society's fundamental interest in limiting litigation, were found to be prohibited by the First Amendment, because suing may be—and, by reason of the Court's purely political constitutional decisions, often is—a form of political speech.[58] The First Amendment severely limits the power of the states to maintain order by regulating marches—even by neo-Nazis in an area with Holocaust survivors—and other public demonstrations, and totally disables the states from prohibiting public burning of the American flag.[59] Even elementary school children are protected from a state's attempt to maintain order in the classroom by prohibiting divisive political displays.[60] The Court's intervention

---

floods of stale, frivolous and repetitious petitions inundate the dockets of the lower courts and swell our own." *Brown v. Allen*, 344 U.S. 443, 536 (1953).

57. *Denver Area Educ. Telecomm. Consortium, Inc. v. FCC*, 518 U.S. 727 (1996) (child pornography); *Schad v. Mount Ephraim*, 452 U.S. 61 (1991) (nude dancing); *Cohen v. California*, 403 U.S. 15 (1971) (vulgarity).

58. *NAACP v. Button*, 371 U.S. 415 (1963).

59. *Village of Skokie v. Nat'l Soc. Party of Am.*, 69 Ill.2d 605, 373 N.E.2d 21 (1978) (Nazis); *Cox v. Louisiana*, 379 U.S. 536 (1965) (public demonstration); *Texas v. Johnson*, 491 U.S. 397 (1989) (flag burning).

60. *Tinker v. Des Moines School Dist.*, 393 U.S. 503 (1969).

in the running of the nation's public schools, the effect of which has been to seriously impair school discipline and the ability of teachers to teach, should be enough to illustrate the danger of giving the Court the final word on matters about which it can know very little.[61]

At the height of the Cold War, the "First Amendment" denied the federal government the power to exclude Communist Party members from working in defense plants and denied the states the power to exclude them as teachers in public schools.[62] The American Communist Party, the justices, led by Douglas and Black, insisted, reflecting a central and unshakable liberal belief, was an organization of loyal Americans fighting for "social justice," not, as proved the case, a tool of the Soviet Union. Proving the justices wrong on issues where they can be proven wrong never serves, of course, to shake their confidence in the superiority of their insights. The Court has remade, or unmade, libel law, overthrowing traditional notions of the importance of protecting reputation.[63] It has contributed substantially to the deterioration of the quality of life in our cities by seeing only oppression in traditional vagrancy control ordinances. "[P]oor people, nonconformists, dissenters, idlers," Justice Douglas instructed, cannot "be required to comport themselves according to the lifestyle deemed appropriate" by public authorities.[64] City dwellers may have reason to disagree, but their municipal governments cannot argue with the First Amendment.

The failure of the proposed Equal Rights Amendment—which would have equated sex discrimination with race discrimination— to gain adoption in the political process was taken by the justices

61. See Heather MacDonald, "Unsafe at Any Grade," Wall St. J., March 25, 2004, p. D6, reviewing Richard Arum, Judging School Discipline (2003) and Elizabeth Gold (2003), Brief Intervals of Horrible Sanity: "How did things get so bad? Blame one of the most ill-conceived chapters of 1960s legal activism."

62. United States v. Robel, 389 U.S. 258 (1917) (defense plants); Elfbrandt v. Russell, 384 U.S. 11 (1966) (schools).

63. See, e.g., Curtis Publishing v. Butts, 338 U.S. 130 (1967).

64. Papachristou v. Jacksonville, 405 U.S. 156, 170 (1972).

as evidence of another defect in the process that required their remedy. It had already been adopted, the Court in effect declared in a series of decisions, by ratification of the Fourteenth Amendment, illustrating how much easier it is to amend the Constitution by a Supreme Court decision than by the onerous and contentious constitutional process. The Court, in an opinion by Justice Brennan, came within one vote of enacting the Equal Rights Amendment in all but name by equating sex and race discrimination.[65] A state may not, the Court held in an opinion by Justice Sandra Day O'Connor, operate a nursing school for women even though it operated a co-ed nursing school as well.[66] Not even a military school, the Court held in an opinion by Justice Ruth Bader Ginsburg, may operate as an all-male institution consistently with the Fourteenth Amendment.[67]

By disallowing nearly all distinctions based on alienage or illegitimacy, the Court has made American law probably unique in both respects.[68] In no other country can the distinction between citizenship and alienage and between legitimacy and illegitimacy be less important. The Court has ordered the redistricting of all political entities, state and federal, on a "one-person, one-vote" basis, excepting only the United States Senate[69]—existence of which might be taken to show that the framers did not share the Court's view.

In each of these important, if not revolutionary, decisions the Court, without exception, held unconstitutional a policy choice made in the ordinary political process, reflecting traditional values, only to substitute an innovative policy further to the political left. It would be difficult to find a decision of comparable importance

65. *Frontiero v. Richardson*, 411 U.S. 677 (1973).
66. *Mississippi University for Women v. Hogan*, 458 U.S. 718 (1982).
67. *United States v. Virginia*, 518 U.S. 515 (1996).
68. *Graham v. Richardson*, 403 U.S. 365 (1971) (alienage); *Levy v. Louisiana*, 391 U.S. 68 (1968) (illegitimacy).
69. *Reynolds v. Sims*, 377 U.S. 533 (1964).

during the same period that had the opposite effect. In the guise of enforcing the Constitution, the Court faithfully enacted the political program of the liberal cultural elite, working a thoroughgoing revolution in American law and life.

The Myth of a Conservative Supreme Court

But, liberal academics and media are constantly telling us, while it may be true that the Court's rulings of unconstitutionality have for some decades enacted the Left's political agenda—that now is history. The role of the Court has been drastically changed, if not reversed, the public is led to believe, beginning in 1986 under the "Rehnquist Court," which is at least as activist in the service of conservative causes as its two immediate predecessors, the Warren (1959–1969) and Burger (1969–1986) Courts, were in the service of liberal causes.[70] This claim has been so confidently and frequently asserted as to become, at least in the liberal media, conventional wisdom, despite the fact that the Court's rulings of unconstitutionality continue overwhelmingly to favor liberal causes.

The public's view of the Court necessarily comes mainly from the media, and the media's view mainly from liberal academics. For a Court to be considered conservative in liberal academia, it is not necessary that it give conservatives positive victories similar to those it gives liberals—by holding, for example, that abortion is not only not constitutionally protected, overruling *Roe v. Wade*, but

---

70. According to two prominent constitutional law scholars: "[C]onservative judicial activism is the order of the day. The Warren Court was retiring compared with the present one." NYU law professor Larry Kramer, "No Surprise It's an Activist Court," *N.Y. Times*, Dec. 12, 2000, at A33; "We are now in the midst of a remarkable period of right-wing judicial activism. The Supreme Court has moderates but no liberals." University of Chicago law professor Cass Sunstein, "Tilting the Scales Rightward," *N. Y. Times*, April 26, 2001, at A23.

is constitutionally prohibited. Nor is it even necessary that the Court rescind some earlier liberal victories by, for example, over-ruling *Miranda* or the prayer decisions. It is quite enough that the liberal victories come less quickly or surely, and it is unacceptable, an abuse of judicial power, that there should be an occasional positive conservative victory. A half-century of consistent liberal victories has made them seem the normal and appropriate result of the Court's rulings of unconstitutionality, virtually the point of constitutional law.

Because conservatives, by definition, seek to preserve rather than uproot traditional practices and values, they are much less in need than liberals of constitutional victories, and they have, in any event, been granted very few by the Rehnquist Court. The Burger Court, to the disappointment of opponents of the Warren Court revolution and to the surprise of nearly everyone, was, as the title of a book on the subject put it, "the counter-revolution that wasn't."[71] Rather than overruling the major victories that the Warren Court gave liberals, the Burger Court gave them more, and sometimes even more radical, victories of its own. It was the Burger, not the Warren, Court that, for example, first prohibited sex discrimination, created a constitutional right to an abortion, and ordered busing for school racial balance.[72] The Rehnquist Court has failed to overturn the major liberal victories of either the Warren or the Burger Court.[73] Instead, it has accepted them as legiti-

71. *The Burger Court: The Counter-Revolution That Wasn't* (Vincent Blasi ed. 1983).

72. *Roe v. Wade*, 410 U.S. 113 (1973) (abortion); *Swann v. Charlotte-Mecklenburg Bd. of Educ.*, 402 U.S. 1 (1971) (busing); *Reed v. Reed*, 404 U.S. 71 (1971) (sex discrimination).

73. *Employment Division v. Smith*, 494 U.S. 872 (1990), in effect overruling *Sherbert v. Verner*, 374 U.S. 398 (1963), a Brennan opinion creating a religious exemption from the application of ordinary law (which, however, had almost never been followed) is an exception. Ironically, Congress then attempted to overrule *Smith* by the so-called Religious Freedom Restoration Act of 1993, which the Court, insisting on

mate additions to the Constitution, available as springboards for still further liberal advances.

The Rehnquist Court not only failed to overrule *Roe v. Wade*, as it was expected to do, but extended it to protect even so-called partial-birth abortions.[74] It not only failed to overrule the prayer in the schools decisions but extended them to prohibit even a non-sectarian evocation of the deity at a middle-school graduation ceremony.[75] Far from overruling or even relaxing the Burger Court's prohibition of sex discrimination, the Rehnquist Court extended it to even an all-male military school.[76] The Rehnquist Court failed to overrule *Miranda* and its exclusionary rule and instead held unconstitutional a congressional attempt to limit it.[77] Rather than overruling *Mapp v. Ohio* and its exclusionary rule—excluding evidence obtained by a search the Court deems impermissible—the Court continues to extend it by, for example, excluding evidence obtained by pointing a heat-sensing device at the exterior of a building or by having a drug-sniffing dog walk around an automobile.[78]

The Rehnquist Court held unconstitutional an amendment to the Colorado Constitution adopted by referendum by the people of Colorado to prevent the grant of special rights to homosexuals.[79] It invalidated federal attempts to limit child pornography on the Internet and continued the Court's long-term drive toward the abolition of capital punishment.[80] It invalidated state laws limiting the

---

having the last word, then held unconstitutional. *City of Boerne v. Flores*, 521 U.S. 507 (1997).

74. *Stenberg v. Carhart*, 530 U.S. 914 (2000).

75. *Lee v. Weisman*, 505 U.S. 577 (1992).

76. *United States v. Virginia*, 518 U.S. 515 (1996).

77. *Dickerson v. United States*, 530 U.S. 428 (2000).

78. *Kyllo v. United States*, 533 U.S. 27 (2001) (heat sensor); *City of Indianapolis v. Edmond*, 531 U.S. 32 (2000) (drug-sniffing dog).

79. *Romer v. Evans*, 517 U.S. 620 (1996).

80. *Denver Area Educ. Telecomm. Consortium, Inc. v. FCC*, 918 U.S. 727 (1996)

number of terms their congressional representatives are eligible to serve.[81] Just last term, it invalidated Texas's prohibition of homosexual sodomy and upheld the use of race preferences in granting admission to selective institutions of higher education.[82] If this is a conservative Court, what more could a liberal Court do?

The explanation for the continuing string of important liberal victories from a supposedly conservative Court is that it is misleading to label it, according to convention, as the "Rehnquist Court," as if the chief justice were the dominant figure. Although he can do surprisingly liberal things, such as lead the Court in invalidating Congress's attempt to limit *Miranda*,[83] he is, by today's standard, generally conservative, but he has only one vote. The reality is that the Court has four highly reliable liberal activists, Justices John Paul Stevens, David Souter, Ruth Bader Ginsburg, and Stephen Breyer (in order of seniority, but also, roughly, of their liberal activism), and only three, not quite as reliable, conservatives, the chief justice and Justices Antonin Scalia and Clarence Thomas. To prevail, the conservatives need the votes of both the less predictable Justices Sandra Day O'Connor and Anthony Kennedy, while the liberals need only one, and on basic social policy issues such as in the sodomy decision, one or both is usually available.

The rulings of unconstitutionality favoring conservatives by the Rehnquist Court are few, mostly short lived, and likely to prove relatively unimportant. The principal one is surely the Court's decision in *Bush v. Gore*, ending the vote count in the Florida election and settling the 2000 presidential election.[84] That was undoubtedly

---

(child pornography); *Atkins v. Virginia*, 122 S. Ct. 2242 (2003 (capital punishment); *Ring v. Arizona*, 122 S. Ct. 2428 (2002) (same).

81. *United States Term Limits, Inc. v. Thornton*, 514 U.S. 779 (1995).

82. *Lawrence v. Texas*, 123 S. Ct. 2472 (2003) (sodomy); *Grutter v. Bollinger*, 123 S. Ct. 2325 (2003) (race preferences).

83. *Dickerson v. United States*, 533 U.S. 27 (2001).

84. 531 U.S. 98 (2000).

an activist decision but one dealing with a unique event and arguably justifiable as counteracting the judicial activism of the Florida
Supreme Court. The greatest fear of liberals about the Rehnquist
Court was that it would invalidate, as its precedents seemed to
require, the use of race preferences in making admission decisions
by colleges and universities. With the Court's 2003 decision in
Grutter v. Bollinger, that fear has been removed.[85]

Over the adamant protest of the four consistent liberals, the
Rehnquist Court attempted to reinvigorate the Fifth Amendment's
prohibition ("incorporated" in the Fourteenth Amendment) against
the "taking" of property without just compensation. In a series of
decisions, the Court upheld "regulatory taking" claims, that is,
claims for loss of property values resulting from land-use regulations, rather than from the government taking possession of or
claiming title to the property.[86] This development has now largely
been brought to a halt, if not actually reversed, by the Court's most
recent decision on the issue.[87] Justices O'Connor and Kennedy
both defected to the side of the four consistent liberals to deny a
claim that seemed quite solid under recent prior decisions.

The most discussed and berated example of alleged conservative activism by the Rehnquist Court is some of its decisions on
the federalism issue. The conservatives, usually joined on this issue
by Justices O'Connor and Kennedy, with the liberals always heat-
edly dissenting, have clearly undertaken to protect a degree of state
autonomy from national power. The Court held, in several cases,
that Congress may not authorize certain suits against the states

85. 123 S. Ct. 2472 (2003).
86. *E.g., Dolan v. City of Tigard*, 512 U.S. 374 (1994); *Lucas v. S. C. Coastal
Council*, 505 U.S. 13 (1992); *Nolan v. Cal. Coastal Comm'n*, 483 U.S. 825 (1987);
First English Evangelical Lutheran Church v. County of Los Angeles, 482 U.S. 304
(1987).
87. *Tahoe-Sierra Preservation Council, Inc. v. Tahoe Regional Planning Agency*,
122 S. Ct. 1465 (2002).

without their consent;[88] in two cases, that Congress may not require the states to cooperate in certain ways in the enforcement of federal law;[89] and most strikingly, in two cases, that Congress may not regulate certain noncommercial activities on the basis of the commerce clause.[90]

The Court's most recent decision on the issue of suits against the states indicates, like the latest case on the regulatory taking issue, that the movement has been brought to a halt or even cut back.[91] On the compulsory cooperation issue, Congress can usually prevail by simply placing conditions on federal monetary grants.[92] The Court's two decisions invalidating purported exercises of the commerce power are likely to prove more a matter of form than substance. The Court has gone out of its way to emphasize that Congress may achieve noncommercial ("police power") objectives through the commerce power, providing it does so by placing restrictions on the interstate movement of people or goods.[93] In sum, with few deviations, not likely to prove important, and almost no steps backward, the Rehnquist Court, like the Burger Court, continues on the path of liberal activism set by the Warren Court.

---

88. *Federal Maritime Comm'n v. South Carolina State Ports Auth.*, 535 U.S. 743 (2002); *Kimel v. Florida Bd. of Reports*, 528 U.S. 62 (2000); *Florida Prepaid Postsecondary Educ. Expense Bd. v. Coll. Sav. Bank.* 527 U.S. 666 (1999); *Alden v. Maine*, 527 U.S. 706 (1999); *Seminole Tribe v. Florida*, 517 U.S. 44 (1996).

89. *Printz v. United States*, 521 U.S. 898 (1997); *New York v. United States*, 505 U.S. 144 (1992).

90. *United States v. Lopez*, 514 U.S. 549 (1995); *United States v. Morrison*, 529 U.S. 592 (2000).

91. *Nevada Dep't of Human Resources v. Hibbs*, 123 S. Ct. 1972 (2003).

92. *See, e.g., South Dakota v. Dole*, 483 U.S. 203 (1987).

93. The principal effect of American constitutional federalism, therefore, is to require Congress to do indirectly, by pretense, what it cannot do directly. Congress, for example, clearly has no authority to define sexual crimes—that is exclusively a matter for the states—but Congress can make it a crime to cross a state line for an improper sexual purpose. *See, e.g., Caminetti v. United States*, 242 U.S. 470 (1917).

Judicial Review:
The Trump Card of the Cultural Elite

In the cultural war being fought out in America, the mass of the American people have the numbers, but the cultural elite has judicial review. The nightmare of the elite is that decision making on basic issues of social policy should fall into the hands of the American people. The American people favor capital punishment, restrictions on abortion, prayer in the schools, suppression of pornography, strict enforcement of criminal law, neighborhood schools, and so on, all anathema to the cultural elite. Could anyone really want to live, they wonder, in a society with such policies? Policymaking by a committee of life-tenured lawyers might not be the cultural elite's ideal alternative to popular government—moral philosophers or sociologists, for example, might be better—but it is all that is available. Nothing is more important to them, therefore, than that the power of the Court to invalidate policy choices made in the ordinary political process be defended and preserved.

The dilemma of defenders of judicial review is that it is hardly possible to defend the Court's rulings of unconstitutionality as interpretations of the actual written Constitution in any ordinary sense and even less possible to openly advocate, as an improvement on democratic federalism, policymaking for the nation as a whole by as few as five electorally unaccountable officials. What they attempt, therefore, is to show that though the Court's rulings of unconstitutionality may not exactly be derived from the words of the Constitution, neither are they simply the result of the justices' personal policy preferences; they are the result, instead, of the justices' discovery and disinterested application of universal principles of justice or good government that should prevail whether the people agree with the Court's supposed application of them or not. The ordinarily most secular of scholars become for this purpose advocates of some form of "natural law."

All attempts to make this showing are based on two assertions, both mistaken. The first is that there are authoritative, preexisting, and objectively discernible principles—apart from the Constitution or any enacted law—that provide, although perhaps only to the exceptionally skilled and only after Herculean effort, objectively "correct" resolutions of difficult social policy issues.[94] The second is that Supreme Court justices, perhaps aided by the work of constitutional scholars, can be trusted, more than other government officials can, to possess the skill needed to discover these principles and the integrity to apply them in a disinterested manner.

These theories are similar to Plato's argument for rule by philosopher kings, persons of exceptional wisdom, integrity, and erudition, but not even Plato, presumably, would favor rule by lawyer kings. As one would go to an expert cabinetmaker to have a good cabinet made, the theory is, one should go to social policy experts to have good social policies made. The theory of democracy, however, repeatedly confirmed by experience, is that there are no superior beings—there's nobody here but us—to whom ordinary people can safely delegate final decision-making power about how they should live. "For myself it would be most irksome," the great judge Learned Hand objected to the Supreme Court activism of his day, "to be ruled by a bevy of Platonic Guardians, even if I knew how to choose them, which I assuredly do not."[95] It is even more irksome to be ruled by lawyer guardians who must pretend to reach their policy decisions by studying—as witch doctors do the entrails of birds—the Constitution.

A problem of social choice is a problem not because we have difficulty discovering the resolving principle but because we have many principles, and they, like the interests they represent, inevitably come into conflict. There is no way to resolve the problem

---

94. *See, e.g.*, Ronald Divorkin, *Taking Rights Seriously* (1977).
95. Learned Hand, *The Bill of Rights* (1958).

except by evaluating the conflicting interests and making some sort of compromise or trade-off, usually sacrificing each interest to some extent to the other. For example, parades may be a valuable form of political expression, but they unavoidably impede the flow of traffic. As an economist would put it, these conflicting interests cannot simultaneously be maximized. The conflict cannot be resolved purely by logic or empirical investigation but only by a policy choice evaluating the relative importance of unimpeded traffic flow and of this form of political expression at the particular time and place. The essence of democracy is that these judgments are to be made by the people affected or by their elected representatives. Leaving the decision to the Supreme Court instead does not produce a "better" decision but only one almost surely more in accord with elite policy preferences. In the stated example, the speech interest will be evaluated very highly—speaking is what the cultural elite do—and the inconveniences and losses involved—which members of the elite are often in a position to avoid—very much less so.

The second assertion, that Supreme Court justices are people of exceptional skill and integrity as policy analysts, with no personal interest in the resolution of policy issues, is, if anything, even more clearly mistaken. The justices are, for two reasons, the least likely public officials to make informed, disinterested decisions on public policy issues. First, their only professional qualification is that they must be lawyers, professionally skilled in the manipulation of language to achieve a predetermined result. Nothing in the study or practice of law is calculated to inculcate exceptional candor, ethical refinement, or habits of intellectual integrity. The study or practice of law is more likely to inculcate the ability to blur the distinction between truth and falsehood and to accommodate the mind to the untroubled assertion of fiction.

It is not likely that many Supreme Court justices strongly committed to a result have felt themselves unable to reach it because they lacked the lawyerly linguistic or rhetorical skills necessary to overcome some impediment of law, fact, or logic.[96] Consider, for example, the opinions of Justices Brennan, Marshall, and Blackmun on the unconstitutionality of capital punishment,[97] the opinion of Justice Ginsburg on the unconstitutionality of an all-male military school,[98] the opinion of Justice O'Connor upholding racial discrimination by a state university in the face of *Brown* and of Title VI of the 1964 Civil Rights Act's explicit prohibition,[99] or for that matter, the Court's latest opinion justifying a ruling of unconstitutionality.

Second, Supreme Court justices are the public officials least to be trusted to make policy decisions on any basis other than personal preference, for the further and more fundamental reason that they are the public officials least accountable to the public or otherwise subject to external control. It is not that they are morally inferior beings but only that they are human beings, no more exempt than others from the corrupting effect of uncontrolled power. Power corrupts less by making men (and women) venal than by distorting their judgment. It is apparently bad for the human soul to be always obeyed and freed from contradiction. The result seems inevitably to be an exaggerated view of one's knowledge, wisdom, and benevolence and a narrow view as to the possible possession of those qualities by others. One cannot study the Court's opinions justifying rulings of unconstitutionality without being struck by the authors' extraordinary confidence in their own wisdom and goodness, as well as by their distrust of their fellow citizens and their consequent lack of compunction in imposing their views on those who disagree.

---

96. In fact, the revival of explicit substantive due process that began with *Griswold* means that the making of constitutional law without or despite the Constitution requires no more than a willingness to assert that the opposite of the favored result would be "unreasonable."

97. *Supra*, n. 47.

98. *United States v. Virginia*, 518 U.S. 515 (1996).

99. *Grutter v. Bollinger*, 123 S. Ct. 2325 (2003).

The justices clearly operate on the assumption, common to wielders of uncontrolled power, that their undoubted good intentions grant them exemption from the obligations of honesty and good faith applicable to other public officials. This is nowhere more clear than in their decisions on race, the area that is the basis of the modern Court's power and prestige. In the 1964 Civil Rights Act, Congress in effect ratified what it understood to be *Brown*'s prohibition of all official racial discrimination, made it effective as to the assignment of students to schools (Title IV), and expanded it to apply to all institutions that receive federal funds (Title VI) and even to private employers (Title VII). The history of race discrimination law since the Act is a hardly believable (at least for nonlawyers) history of the Court standing each of these titles on its head, converting them—exactly as Southern opponents of the Act feared and as proponents insisted could never happen—from prohibitions of race discrimination to permission for, or even requirements of, race discrimination.

The end of compulsory racial segregation did not mean, it soon appeared, the end of all racial separation; it was time, therefore, the Court concluded—riding a crest of moral fervor and urged on by the "civil rights" establishment that had grown up after *Brown*— to move on to compulsory integration by law. The law of race discrimination with which we struggle today derives not from *Brown's* prohibition of segregation, but from the Court's far more ambitious and questionable 1968 decision in *Green v. County School Board* to impose, without admitting it, a requirement of integration.[100] The South had no sooner finally been made to comply with *Brown*'s prohibition of racial discrimination, because of the 1964 Act, than it was required to begin racially discriminating again, now to increase school racial integration or balance. For several reasons, the Court could not make this move openly. For

100. 391 U.S. 430 (1968).

one thing, it would be expected to explain the benefits of compulsory integration, something it has never attempted to do. More important, the requirement would have applied at once not just to the South but to the racial separation that exists in the school systems of all our major cities, which would have caused massive national resistance to the decision. The Court imposed it, instead, in the North and West one city or area at a time, which operated to avoid unified opposition. Perhaps most important, the Court would have had to overrule or at least qualify what everyone, including the Congress, understood to be the nondiscrimination principle of *Brown*—the last thing the Court wanted to do.

That the Court could not make the move to compulsory integration openly did not stop it from making the move. The Court explicitly denied that it was imposing a requirement of integration in *Green* but imposed the requirement nonetheless by holding unconstitutional a racially imbalanced school system that concededly had ended all racial discrimination. The only requirement, the Court insisted, was "desegregation," nothing more than the requirement of *Brown*. "Desegregation," however, now meant not ending but practicing racial assignment. To this day, the Court insists that there is no constitutional requirement of integration or racial balance—that one-race schools are not unconstitutional—even while ordering that students be bused across citywide school districts that, like Denver's, were never segregated, in order to increase racial balance.[101] Rather than having to reverse *Brown*, the Court was thus able to wrap itself in the protective mantle of *Brown*, performing the feat, possible only for an institution both subject to no review and unscrupulous, of requiring racial discrimination in the name of prohibiting it.[102] The restraining power of law—rules stated in words—is entirely dependent on the good faith of the

101. *Keyes v. School District*, 413 U.S. 189 (1973).
102. For a full discussion see Lino A. Graglia, *Disaster by Decree: The Supreme Court Decisions on Race and the Schools* (1976).

interpreters of the words, and good faith has been entirely absent from many of the Court's decisions on race.

Chief Justice Warren Burger—newly appointed by President Nixon, who ran for president as an opponent of racial busing—tried to get the Court to state honestly the meaning of "desegregation" and the "nonracial unitary system" that was supposedly the constitutional requirement. Justice Brennan successfully prevented the Court from doing so by arguing that for it to openly state that the actual constitutional requirement was not desegregation but simply integration "would, given the views of most whites, simply be impractical."[103] When honesty is impractical for the justices to achieve their objective, they can and do simply turn to its alternative. School boards would continue to be told that they were required to operate nonracial school systems, while at the same time being ordered to assign students to schools by race.

Another difficulty faced by the Court in imposing a requirement of school racial integration in the name of desegregation is that this requirement is precisely what Congress was most concerned to avoid in enacting Title IV of the 1964 Act. Opponents of Title IV insisted, correctly, that zealous judges and bureaucrats would not be satisfied with Congress's purpose to make *Brown*'s prohibition of segregation by law a reality, and would seek, instead, to move to forced integration. Senator Hubert Humphrey, floor manager of the bill in the Senate, dismissed their fears as "bogeymen and hobgoblins" and undertook to give opponents every assurance that what they feared could not happen.[104]

After all, Senator Humphrey pointed out, Title IV defines "desegregation" as "the assignment of students to public schools . . . without regard to their race," and in a seeming excess of

103. See Lino A. Graglia, *"When Honesty Is 'Simply . . . Impractical' for the Supreme Court: How the Constitution Came to Require Busing for School Racial Balance,"* 85 Mich. L. Rev. 1193 (1987).
104. 110 Cong. Rec. 6552 (1964).

caution, repeats that it "shall not mean the assignment of students to public schools in order to overcome racial imbalance."[105] What could be clearer than that? The prohibition is then repeated twice more in Title IV.[106] As the ultimate assurance to skeptical southern senators, Senator Humphrey stated that Congress could not impose a requirement of busing for school racial balance even if it wanted to, because that would be a constitutional "violation, because it would be handling the matter on the basis of race and we would be transporting children because of race."[107]

All to no avail. In 1971 in *Swann v. Charlotte-Mecklenburg Board of Education*, a unanimous Court blandly asserted, with no citation to the Congressional Record, that the definition of "desegregation" as nonracial assignment, and not as assignment to overcome racial imbalance, was not meant to apply to the formerly segregated school systems of the South, the only place where, Congress thought, a requirement of desegregation could be applied.[108] As Senator Sam Ervin of North Carolina, considered the Senate's leading constitutionalist at the time, commented:

> [T]he Congress decided to take no chances with the courts, so it put in something else that even a judge ought to be able to understand. It not only defined "desegregation," affirmatively, but also defined what "desegregation" is not. The Supreme Court adopted exactly the opposite interpretation of the meaning of the word "desegregation." . . . [T]he Supreme Court nullified this act of Congress by holding that Congress was a bunch of legislative fools. . . .[109]

In *Regents of the University of California v. Bakke*, the Court

105. 42 U.S.C. sec.202000c (2003), 78 Stat. 246.
106. 42 U.S.C. secs. 2000c-6(a)(2), 2000c-9 (2003), 78 Stat. 248, 249.
107. 110 Cong. Rec. 12717 (1964).
108. 402 U.S. 1 (1971).
109. "Busing of School Children, Hearings Before the Subcommittee on Constitutional Rights of the Committee on the Judiciary, United States Senate," 93d Cong. 2d Sess. [1974], 42–43.

similarly held that Title VI's prohibition of racial discrimination by institutions receiving federal funds was not violated by the practice—by a state university that received federal funds—of racially discriminating in granting or denying admission.[110] In *Griggs v. Duke Power Co.*, a unanimous Court effectively converted Title VII's prohibition of racial discrimination into a requirement of discrimination by holding that Congress meant to forbid an employer's use of such ordinary employment criteria as a verbal test or a high school education when the effect was to disproportionately disqualify blacks.[111] In fact, Congress had specifically considered the issue, and made it clear that employers acting in good faith were free to set qualifications as high as they wished regardless of disproportionate racial effects.[112] It is unlikely that any public officials other than Supreme Court justices could engage in comparable acts of malfeasance and bad faith without being subject to serious sanction.

"[N]o one—absolutely no one," not even the president, Special Prosecutor Leon Jaworski proudly asserted, when President Nixon was forced to succumb to a Supreme Court order that he release his infamous tapes, "is above its law."[113] A more accurate statement of what the incident illustrated would be that even the president is subject to the Supreme Court. But to whom, Jaworski unfortunately did not go on to inquire, is the Supreme Court subject? No one issues orders to it or reverses its decisions, and espe-

110. 438 U.S. 265 (1978).

111. 401 U.S. 424 (1971).

112. Senators Case and Clark, co-managers of the bill that became Title VII, stated in an authoritative memorandum that Title VII "expressly protects the employer's right to insist that any prospective applicant, Negro or white, must meet the applicable job qualifications," 110 Cong. No. 7247 (1964), and in an earlier memorandum, "There is no requirement in Title VII that the employer abandon bona fide qualification tests where . . . members of some groups are able to perform better on those tests than members of other groups." 110 Cong. Rec. 7213 (1964).

113. Leon Jaworski, *The Right and the Power* 279 (1976).

cially in constitutional cases, it is not only above the law but its decisions, it insists, are the law.[114]

Bishop Hoadly famously pointed out to the King of England in 1717 that "[w]hoever hath an absolute authority to interpret any written or spoken laws, it is he who is truly the lawgiver, to all intents and purposes, and not the person who first spoke or wrote them." Charles Evans Hughes, later chief justice, made the same point in a speech in 1907: "We are under a Constitution, but the Constitution is what the judges say it is."[115] Which is to say, of course, that we are under only the Court, and the Court is under no one. Power without accountability is the definition of tyranny, and even good people when made tyrants take on characteristics of tyrants. Tocqueville has been proven correct in that the Supreme Court is not the least, as Hamilton argued, but the most dangerous branch of the national government, such that if it "is ever composed of imprudent or bad men, the Union may be plunged into anarchy or civil war,"[116] which, of course, is exactly what happened.

The Means of Limiting the Supreme Court's Power

The means of limiting the power of the Supreme Court and returning the nation to the constitutional plan of democratic federalism clearly exist in theory. The justices, after all, number only nine and control, as Hamilton pointed out in defense of judicial review, neither the sword nor the purse, implying that those who do may use them, if need be, to control the Court. Finding the will to use them is another matter. Most Americans and, apparently even more so,

---

114. *See, e.g., Cooper v. Aaron*, 358 U.S. 1 (1958) ("the federal judiciary is supreme in the exposition of the Constitution," and the Court's interpretation of the Constitution "is the supreme law of the land").

115. Quoted in Jesse H. Choper et al., *The American Constitution* 1, 8 (9th ed., 2001).

116. *Supra*, p. 1.

their political leaders have become so thoroughly accustomed or resigned to leaving basic social policy decisions to the Court that it seems to have become part of the natural order and taken on aspects of a religious faith. The Constitution is our holiest scripture, but rather than therefore fiercely defending it against the Court's desecrations, we have allowed ourselves to accept the Court as its oracle. Liberal legal academia has largely succeeded in establishing that blunt criticism of the Court is an attack on both judicial independence and—like noting the emperor's nakedness—a necessary public faith. The result is that we have allowed a handful of electorally unaccountable public officials, acting in the name of protecting our constitutional rights, to deprive us of our most important right, the right of self-government.

If the Court's decisions on, for example, abortion (converting an issue that was being peacefully settled on a state-by-state basis, generally in favor of liberalization, into an intractable issue inflaming national politics) or forced busing (devastating the nation's public school systems at the cost of billions of dollars for no benefit) were not enough for the people to demand and for Congress to take action to curb the Court's power, it is hard to see what could be.[117] Democracy is not self-preserving; it can be ended by popular vote or, as here, by the failure of elected representatives to protest as issue after issue of basic social policy is removed from their control. The crux of the problem, as already noted, is that the cultural elite distrusts and fears popular rule, much preferring rule by the Court; and the elite dominates communication and education.

Justices can, of course, be impeached, which Hamilton saw as a "complete security" against misuse of the power of judicial

---

117. In carrying out a single federal district judge's orders, billions of dollars were spent on Kansas City, Missouri's school system alone. See *Missouri v. Jenkins*, 515 U.S. 70 (1995). How much would a federal judge have to order spent, one must wonder, before he met resistance—ten billion, one hundred billion?

review. Sufficient ground for impeachment, as then Representative Gerald Ford said about the attempted impeachment of Justice Douglas, is "whatever a majority of the House of Representatives considers [it] to be,"[118] Congress apparently having on this, if on little else, the last word. A justice's demonstrable deliberate dishonesty in the performance of judicial duty would, in a system insisting on judicial integrity, be grounds enough. By this standard, very few justices of the past fifty years would not have had short careers. It would seem that the justices can hardly be impeached, however, for continuing to do—though at an accelerating pace—what they have always been known and permitted to do; they must at least be given notice that a certain minimum level of integrity will be required from now on. In any event, impeachment is a crude, disputable, and unseemly means of remedying judicial misbehavior.

The Constitution provides that the Supreme Court exercise appellate jurisdiction subject to "such Exceptions and under such Regulations as the Congress shall make."[119] Theoretically, Congress could use this power to virtually take the Court out of the business of manufacturing constitutional law, leaving it with only the very limited original jurisdiction granted it by the Constitution. Attempting to limit the Court's power by laws restricting its jurisdiction is subject, however, to the Catch-22 problem that the constitutionality of the laws will itself be subject to judicial review, with the result that the attempt will be successful only to the extent that the Court permits.[120] Use of the power would also leave the Court's activist rulings of unconstitutionality standing and very likely to be followed by other courts. Congress can presumably also limit the jurisdiction of the lower federal courts, which it cre-

---

118. 116 Cong. Rec. 11, 913 (1970).

119. U.S. Const. art. III, sec.202.

120. And the Court has not always permitted it, even though the power has been very rarely used. See *United States v. Klein*, 80 U.S. 128 (1972).

ated by statute, but state courts—often at least as activist as the Supreme court—would remain, subject only to such controls as are available to state legislatures.

Congress's use of the jurisdiction-limiting power also has an unfortunate aspect of seeming to win the game by silencing the umpire. The restrictions on abortion and pornography and state-sponsored prayer in schools will be no less unconstitutional, protestors will insist—*e pur se muove* ("and still it moves" legend has Galileo saying when forced to renounce the heliocentric planetary theory)—simply because the Court can no longer declare them so. Despite these problems and although the power has been used so infrequently that its scope is uncertain and disputed, it remains an extremely important power. The Court will surely feel compelled, in the face of a revived and determined Congress, to uphold at least some carefully drafted measures. Any actual exercise of the power by Congress would have the extremely valuable effect, apart from what it actually does, of advising the Court that Congress has at last become seriously concerned with the Court's usurpation of legislative authority and has mustered the political will to do something about it.

Finally, the Court's power can be limited in various ways by a constitutional amendment, even though amendments, too—short of one abolishing judicial review—would be subject to the Court's interpretation. The United States Constitution is, however, exceedingly difficult to amend, perhaps the most difficult of any developed nation's. An amendment must be proposed by a vote of at least two-thirds of each house of Congress or at least two-thirds of the states meeting in a convention and, in either case, then ratified by three-quarters of the states.[121] Disapproval by one-third plus one of the members of either House of Congress or by one legislative body in one-quarter plus one of the states would be sufficient to defeat it. The amendment process does very little to reconcile gov-

---

121. U.S. Const. art. V.

ernment by judges with democracy. It was apparently thought that its use would rarely be necessary, but the framers could not have foreseen that the result would be a system of government by judges who can be highly confident that their decisions, no matter how harmful and unwanted by the people, will not be overturned.

A frequently suggested amendment would eliminate life tenure for Supreme Court justices, limiting their terms of office to, for example, twelve or sixteen years. The result would be to ensure or nearly ensure that each newly elected president made one or more appointments to the Court. President Bush has not yet made an appointment to the Court; President Clinton, like President Reagan, during two terms in office was able to make only two. Along with life tenure, the robe today seems to confer longevity, and few justices do not exhaust it; presidents leave office after four or eight years while their appointees to the Court remain over three or four decades. Lifetime judicial tenure may have had more to be said for it when the average life span was forty or fifty years. The present Court has remained unchanged in membership for over ten years.

Other suggestions include selecting the justices by election, usually for a fixed term, rather than by appointment, and requiring that rulings of unconstitutionality be by a unanimous, or at least more than majority, vote. These, like almost any amendment seeking to limit the power of the Court, are likely to be highly beneficial, if only because they at least demonstrate a popular and political awareness that there is a problem needing correction and a willingness to act. The same may be said of proposed amendments to overturn particular Supreme Court rulings of unconstitutionality. The Court's decision that public burning of the American flag is constitutionally protected "speech," for example, may not be among its most socially harmful decisions, but overturning it by constitutional amendment would, again, at least provide a much needed demonstration that the Court need not on every issue have the last word.

None of these proposed amendments would, however, address

the root problem of judicial review. Electing justices and limiting their term of office would not eliminate the Court's policymaking power or its inconsistency with the constitutional scheme, though success in obtaining an amendment would no doubt cause the justices, at least at first, to be more cautious in its exercise. It is conceivable, however, that having only a limited term of office, appointed or elected, might be seen by some justices as all the more reason to act quickly and decisively while they can. Requiring a supermajority or even unanimous vote for rulings of unconstitutionality should reduce, but would certainly not eliminate, unjustifiable invalidations. The dishonest and indefensible *Green* and *Swann* decisions, for example (as well as *Griggs*, a statutory case) were decided unanimously.

Robert H. Bork has made the valuable suggestion of a constitutional amendment authorizing Congress to overturn Supreme Court constitutional decisions by a supermajority vote. This would undoubtedly be a significant limitation on the Court's power, as it would create a realistic possibility of elected legislators having the last word on fundamental social policy issues, a minimum requirement of democratic government. Because it is much easier to defeat than to enact legislation, however, the Court would as a practical matter still often have the last word, and all the more so, of course, to the extent that more than a majority vote in Congress is required. The amendment would nonetheless make so great an improvement in our present situation that it should be fully and enthusiastically supported by opponents of rule by the Court, especially in the very unlikely event that it should appear to have any chance of being adopted.

The surest and most complete—and therefore least likely to be adopted—response to the usurpation of legislative power by judges is, of course, a constitutional amendment simply abolishing judicial review. The result would be to return the nation to the experiment in popular self-government with which it began and make a strong statement of renewed self-confidence by the American people in their ability to govern themselves without the guidance, supervision, and permission of their supposed moral and intellectual superiors. All that is needed to support the move is agreement with Churchill that imperfect as democracy may be, it is less so than all the other forms of government that have been tried. Whatever the best form of government, surely government by majority vote of nine unelected, life-tenured lawyers pretending to interpret the Constitution is one of the worst.

A much less drastic constitutional amendment, fortunately, is likely to be almost as effective and more difficult to oppose. As noted above, it is not judge-enforced constitutionalism, as such, but judicial activism, rulings of unconstitutionality not based on the Constitution, that gives the Court its ruling power. Whatever might be said for real constitutionalism—judicial enforcement of meaningful constitutional provisions—as an aid to or improvement on democracy, there would seem to be nothing to be said for constitutionalism without the Constitution, for treating constitutional provisions as meaningless except as transfers of policymaking power to judges.

Because the Court's activism is very largely based on what the Court has made of the Fourteenth Amendment—rendering the due process and equal protection clauses empty vessels into which it can pour any meaning—a very large part of the answer to the problem of rule by the Court would be simply to return the Fourteenth Amendment to its intended meaning or to give it any specific meaning. If Representative Thaddeus Stevens, leader of the Radical Republicans in the House, and other proponents of full legal equality for the newly freed blacks had had their way, the Fourteenth Amendment would have simply prohibited all official racial discrimination. Concern that such an amendment would not be ratified (and would lead to the defeat of Republicans in the coming election), because of northern opposition to giving blacks the right to vote, resulted in rejection of the proposal and in adoption instead of the first section of the Fourteenth Amendment in its present, much more elaborate form.[122] If interpreted to mean what it was intended to mean, it would, as noted above, guarantee blacks basic "civil" (but not "political") rights. The right to vote was granted to blacks, however, two years later with the adoption of the Fifteenth Amendment, effectively abolishing the civil-political distinction. There is much to be said, therefore, for returning the Fourteenth Amendment to the clear, appealing, and easily administratable meaning that Representative Stevens intended, a simple prohibition of all official racial discrimination. This is the interpretation the Court adopted in one of its earliest and most important decisions under the amendment.[123]

Returning the Fourteenth Amendment to a specific meaning would very largely end extraconstitutional judicial review and, therefore, rulings of unconstitutionality against state laws. Doing so should be easy to support, and difficult to oppose, on the ground that if it is constitutionalism we truly want, not government by judges, it is necessary to have a Constitution with meaning. The Supreme Court would still be able in theory to enforce its imaginative interpretations of the first eight amendments against federal law, but Congress would be much more likely to assert itself if it became nearly the sole victim of the Court's interventions. The Court, too, would undoubtedly find reasons for restraint in the face of a demonstrated public resolve to limit judicial power by reestablishing a Constitution with meaning.

In sum, if opponents of government by judges should ever gain sufficient political strength to obtain a constitutional amendment, they should not use it merely to tinker with the method of selecting Supreme Court justices or of deciding their term of office or with

122. *See, e.g.*, Charles Fairman, *Reconstruction and Reunion: 1864–1888, Part One* 7 (1971).
123. *Strauder v. West Virginia*, 100 U.S. 303 (1879).

the requirement of a supermajority vote for rulings of unconstitutionality. They should use it, ideally, to abolish judicial review altogether, or at least to give Congress the last word on constitutional questions. Most easily defended and perhaps politically feasible—if any Court-limiting proposal can be—would be simply to give the Fourteenth Amendment a specific meaning. Such a change would amount to little more than a requirement that the justices use the power of judicial review honestly, do only what they purport, and are supposedly authorized, to do, and disallow only those policy choices made by the elected representatives of the people that the Constitution in fact disallows. It would reaffirm and reinstitute the federalist system of representative self-government with separation of powers that was created by the Constitution and bring to a halt the Court's continuing assault on American society.

—2—

The
Perverse
Paradox
of Privacy

Gary L. McDowell

It is . . . true that upon no legal principle can an interpretation be supported, which ignores the meaning universally accorded to a word or clause for centuries, and the meaning which must, therefore, have been intended by those who inserted it in the constitution. It is perhaps well to bear this in mind at a time where there is a manifest tendency to regard constitutional prohibitions as a panacea for moral and political evils, to look upon courts of law, as distinguished from legislatures, as the only real protectors of individual rights, and to trust to the courts for remedies for evils resulting entirely from a failure to attend to political duties,—at a time, that is to say, when there is danger of loose and unhistorical constitutional interpretation.
—Charles E. Shattuck, *Harvard Law Review*

The most recent effort of the Supreme Court of the United States to define the judicially created constitutional right to privacy has demonstrated once again why that contrived right poses such a

The author is grateful to Curtis Gannon, Ralph Rossum, and the late James McClellan for their comments and suggestions. This article is respectfully dedicated to the memory of Professor McClellan. *Epigraph:* Charles E. Shattuck, "The True Meaning of the Term 'Liberty' in those Clauses in the Federal and State Constitutions which Protect 'Life, Liberty, and Property,'" *Harvard Law Review* 4 (1891): 365, 366.

58 GARY L. MCDOWELL

pronounced threat to constitutional self-government. In writing for the majority in *Lawrence v. Texas* (2003) to overrule a case of only seventeen years' standing that allowed the states to prohibit homosexual sodomy, Justice Anthony Kennedy insisted that the idea of liberty in the Constitution's due process clauses is not limited to protecting individuals from "unwarranted governmental intrusions into a dwelling or other private places" but has "transcendent dimensions" of a more moral sort.[1] Properly understood, this notion of liberty "presumes an autonomy of self that includes freedom of thought, belief, expression and certain intimate conduct," whether those are mentioned in the Constitution or not.[2] Indeed, had those who originally drafted "the Due Process Clauses of the Fifth and Fourteenth Amendments known the components of liberty in its manifold possibilities, they might have been more specific." But they could not have known since "times can blind us to certain truths and later generations can see that laws once thought necessary and proper in fact serve only to oppress." The essence of the Constitution for Justice Kennedy and his ilk is that it falls to "persons in every generation [to] invoke its principles in their own search for greater freedom."[3] Put more simply, there is nothing permanent in the Constitution, no fundamental, unalterable principles; its meaning comes only from the changing moral views of successive generations of justices.

Justice Kennedy's understanding of the changing metaphysical contours of the right of privacy was drawn in large part from *obiter dictum* in *Planned Parenthood of Southeastern Pennsylvania v. Casey*.[4] In that opinion upholding the abortion decision of *Roe v. Wade* (1973), written by Kennedy along with Justices David Souter and Sandra Day O'Connor, the Court had insisted that lying at the

1. 156 L. Ed. 2d 508 (2003), 515.
2. Ibid.
3. Ibid., 526.
4. 505 U.S. 833 (1992).

heart of the idea of liberty provided in the Constitution "is the right to define one's own concept of existence, of meaning, of the universe, and of the mystery of human life."[5] This was something of a crude echo of a similar *dictum* by Justice Louis Brandeis in his dissent in *Olmstead v. United States* (1928), in which he had rhapsodically insisted that the framers of the Constitution "undertook to secure conditions favorable to the pursuit of happiness. They recognized the significance of man's spiritual nature, of his feelings and of his intellect. They knew that only a part of the pain, pleasure, and satisfactions of life are to be found in material things. They sought to protect Americans in their beliefs, their thoughts, their emotions and their sensations."[6] Because of these views, Brandeis insisted, the framers had "conferred, as against the Government, the right to be let alone—the most comprehensive of rights and the right most valued by civilized men."[7]

The problem is that this "most comprehensive of rights," the judicially discovered "transcendent dimensions" of the meaning of liberty, when embraced by the Court as a ground for judgment, is utterly at odds with the very possibility of constitutional self-government. Such understandings can only be the result of what James Madison once termed "constructive ingenuity,"[8] an ingenuity that seeks to supplant the textual Constitution with the justices' "own moral code," their protests to the contrary notwithstanding.[9]

The paradox of the Supreme Court's constructive ingenuity when it comes to the privacy right is that it is defended in the name of protecting new and often unheard of individual liberties from

5. 410 U.S. 113 (1973); 505 U.S. 833, 851.

6. *Olmstead v. United States*, 277 U.S. 438 (1928), 478.

7. Ibid.

8. James Madison to Robert S. Garnett, February 11, 1824, *Letters and Other Writings of James Madison*, 4 vols. (Philadelphia: J.P. Lippincott, 1865), III: 367–368.

9. *Lawrence v. Texas*, 156 L. Ed. 2d., 521, quoting *Planned Parenthood of Southeastern Pennsylvania v. Casey*, 505 U.S. 833 (1992), 850.

legitimately elected majorities who have passed "laws representing essentially moral choices."[10] But by so restricting the powers of the governments (and this is almost always a restriction on the powers of the governments of the several states) to make such moral choices part of the law, the Court has greatly limited the most important right of individuals, the right to be self-governing, a right that has its roots in the very moral foundations of American republicanism.

The essence of self-government is the right of the people to engage in public deliberation over what is right and what is wrong and to decide how those rights and wrongs are translated into what is deemed legal and illegal. In the end the elevation of a judicially created notion of privacy that can be used to trump nearly every conceivable collective moral judgment made by the people undermines constitutionalism in any meaningful sense. The history alone of the development of the right to privacy exposes its illegitimacy as a matter of constitutional law and demonstrates the danger it poses to that most basic of American political values, the rule of law. For the history shows that with the right to privacy the stability and certainty that the rule of law requires is replaced by political uncertainty and judicial arbitrariness.

A Brief History of a Bad Idea

Although the right to privacy as a matter of constitutional law is of rather recent vintage,[11] the roots of the idea go back much further. Usually, it is understood to have begun with a pioneering law review article, "The Right to Privacy," by Samuel Warren and Louis Brandeis, which appeared in the *Harvard Law Review* in 1890.[12] In fact, there was a longer history of a developing tradition

10. *Bowers v. Hardwick*, 478 U.S. 186, 196 (1986).
11. *Griswold v. Connecticut*, 381 U.S. 479 (1965).
12. Samuel D. Warren and Louis D. Brandeis, "The Right to Privacy," *Harvard Law Review* 4 (1890): 193.

of a privacy right of which that essay was essentially a part.[13] For understanding the current constitutional right of privacy, the most important fact about the argument Warren and Brandeis presented was that it did not advocate expanding the Constitution to protect privacy. It was a more modest effort to create an action in tort law to enable the great and the good to sue for damages when beset by the "continuous ordeal of the camera" or relentless "kodakers" who made the age of yellow journalism all that it could be.[14] Their objective was to "set against the newspapers' jealously guarded first amendment rights a countervailing right on the part of individuals, an explicit 'right to privacy.'"[15]

Warren and Brandeis understood that for such a right to be embraced by "the common law, in its eternal youth," they would have to establish a principled ground for it. Thus their basic argument was that "[p]olitical, social, and economic changes entail the recognition of new rights . . . to meet the demands of society." In the instant case, those changed times demanded "a general right to privacy for thoughts, emotions, and sensations." By their common law calculus, the "general object in view [was] to protect the pri-

13. See Note "The Right to Privacy in Nineteenth Century America," *Harvard Law Review* 94 (1981): 1892–1910.

14. The term "kodakers" was used by the editorial writers at the *New York Times*, as quoted in Denis O'Brien, "The Right of Privacy," *Columbia Law Review* 2 (1902): 437. O'Brien was a member of the New York court that had bucked the state court trend and had denied the extension of the right to privacy in *Roberson v. Rochester Folding Box Co.*, 171 N.Y. 538 (1902), a holding that led to "something of a storm of professional, as well as popular, disapproval." Wilbur Larremore, "The Law of Privacy," *Columbia Law Review* 12 (1912): 693, 694.

Judge O'Brien argued in his law review essay that the "right of privacy . . . is such an intangible thing and conveys such a vague idea that it is doubtful if the law can ever deal with it in any reasonable or practical way." Any court, he further warned, "that will not respect the limitations of the law upon its own powers will not long retain the respect of the people." In the law, he concluded, it is "easy enough to wander away from beaten paths that are safe, but it is not always easy to return." O'Brien, "Right of Privacy," 441, 445, 448.

15. "Right to Privacy in Nineteenth Century America," 1910.

vacy of private life" including the "life, habits, acts, and relations of an individual."[16] The right urged by Warren and Brandeis as a matter of tort law made its way into American law nearly from the beginning, and by the 1960s was widely accepted.[17] But it would also prove to be an idea that would lie dormant and be brought to constitutional life in a way that perhaps neither Warren nor Brandeis might have expected.

Although their argument did not itself contribute to the doctrinal basis of a constitutional right to privacy, Warren and Brandeis were writing at precisely the same moment as were others whose arguments would in time come to support the expansion of the Constitution to include an unwritten right to privacy. The year 1890 was the same year that the Supreme Court inched closer to formally creating the doctrine of substantive due process by which it would invalidate all manner of state laws in the name of economic liberty; for the first time the Court held that a state regulation of railroad rates violated the due process clause of the Fourteenth Amendment. Writing for a divided Court, Justice Samuel Blatchford held that the "reasonableness" of such regulations was "eminently a question for judicial investigation, requiring due process of law for its determination."[18] Perhaps the most striking coincidence was that in the

16. Warren and Brandeis, "Right to Privacy," 193, 206, 215, 216.

17. See Larremore, "Law of Privacy"; see also William Prosser, "Privacy," *California Law Review* 48 (1960): 383.

There had been firm critics, however. One had argued simply and forcefully near the beginning that "the right to privacy does not exist." And the attempt to create it was especially worrying. "That our law is a system that grows and develops in response to the demands of advancing civilization, is due to the fact that new occasions and new circumstances arise which come within the principles upon which our laws were founded; not because new principles and new rights are created to afford that protection or redress which seems to be required." Herbert Spencer Hadley, "The Right to Privacy," *Northwestern Law Review* 3 (1894): 1, 20–21.

18. *Chicago, Milwaukee, and St. Paul Railway Co. v. Minnesota*, 134 U.S. 418 (1890), 458. Three justices dissented noting that such a rate regulation "is a legislative prerogative, not a judicial one," p. 461. This decision would be denounced years later

same volume of the *Harvard Law Review* in which Warren and Brandeis's article "The "Right to Privacy" appeared, another article undertook to sound a warning about the dangers of judges manipulating the meaning of constitutional language—especially the word "liberty" in the due process clauses—through "loose and unhistorical . . . interpretation."[19]

The creation of substantive due process was a development of an older tradition in which some judges were willing to seek meaning beyond the text of the written Constitution. In the earliest days of the republic, one might see an appeal made now and then to natural law or principles of natural justice.[20] Later, the contracts clause of the Constitution provided a way for the Court to find principled meaning in the text that seemed to many to go far beyond the text.[21] These early examples stand out in large measure because there were so few judicial forays beyond the text and arguable intention of the Constitution. In a sense, the generation that knew and understood best the natural law theories of the time saw

---

by Justice Hugo Black for using "the due process clause to protect property rights under natural law concepts." *Adamson v. California*, 332 U.S. 46, 79 (1947).

19. Charles Shattuck, "The True Meaning of the Term 'Liberty' in those Clauses in the Federal and State Constitutions which Protect 'Life, Liberty, and Property,'" *Harvard Law Review* 4 (1891): 365, 366.

20. Justice Samuel Chase in *Calder v. Bull*, for example, argued that legislative acts against "the general principles of law and reason" and at odds with "the great first principles of the social compact" are unconstitutional. 3 U.S. (3 Dall.) 386, 388 (1798).

21. Chief Justice John Marshall, for example, in *Fletcher v. Peck* argued that his decision in that case conformed with "certain great principles of justice, whose authority is universally acknowledged." 10 U.S. 87, 143 (1810). In his only dissent in his entire tenure on the Court, Marshall also saw fit to find arguments outside the text and intention of the Constitution. Individuals, Marshall argued in *Ogden v. Saunders*, do not derive from government their right to contract but bring that right with them into society; that obligation is not conferred on contracts by positive law but is intrinsic and is conferred by the act of the parties. 25 U.S. 213, 346 (1825).

So, too, was Justice Joseph Story willing to appeal to "the principles of natural justice" and "the fundamental laws of every free government" in reaching the decision in *Terrett v. Taylor*, 13 U.S. 43, 52 (1815).

no need to seek in them the grounds of their constitutional decisions.[22] They most assuredly did not see the due process clause of
the Fifth Amendment as a provision pregnant with higher law principles awaiting judicial invocation. Indeed, they understood that
clause and the concept of due process as it had been understood
for hundreds of years: "The words *due process of law* have a precise technical import, and are only applicable to the process and
proceedings of the courts of justice; they can never be referred to
an act of the legislature."[23]

It is more than slightly ironic that the doctrine that came to be
a primary vehicle for the Supreme Court of the United States to
invalidate state laws with which the justices disagreed would have
its first appearance in a state court; it is perhaps even more ironic
that the doctrine appeared in the same state in which Alexander
Hamilton had explained the limits of due process of law so clearly,
and that the doctrine was created to stem the tide of judicial reliance on "theories alleged to be found in natural reason and inal-
ienable rights."[24] But that was the situation in 1856, in *Wynehamer
v. New York*, when a court for the first time held that legislation
could be invalidated if its substantive provisions conflicted with
what was demanded by the "due process of law." The state law in
question that sought to prohibit liquor was too arbitrary and unreasonable to stand; but it would fall not because it was "contrary to
natural equity or justice" or violated "any fanciful theory of higher

22. See Henry Steele Commager, "Constitutional History and the Common Law,"
in *The Constitution Reconsidered*, ed. Conyers Read (New York: Columbia University
Press, 1938).

23. Alexander Hamilton in the New York Assembly commenting on the New
York Constitution, February 6, 1787, in Harold C. Syrett, ed., *The Papers of Alexander Hamilton*, 26 vols. (New York: Columbia University Press, 1961–1979), IV:
35.

24. The reliance on such theories, Justice Comstock argued, was "subversive of
the just and necessary powers of government." *Wynehamer v. New York*, 13 N.Y. 378
(1856), 391.

law or first principles of natural rights outside the constitution."[25] It was invalid, the court ruled, because such laws violated the clear text of the state constitution; they were against what was demanded by due process of law.

At the federal level, the first flirtation by the Supreme Court with the idea of substantive due process came the year after *Wynehamer* in the case of *Dred Scott v. Sandford*.[26] In Chief Justice Roger Taney's view, "the rights of property are united with the rights of the person, and placed on the same ground by the fifth amendment to the Constitution, which provides that no person shall be deprived of life, liberty, and [*sic*] property, without due process of law." Such an act of Congress that deprived Mr. Sandford of his property simply because he had taken his slave into a particular territory "could hardly be dignified with the name of due process of law."[27] With the end of the Civil War and the adoption of the Fourteenth Amendment, this nascent notion would find a new and expansive constitutional field.

At first, the Supreme Court resisted the temptation to infuse the due process clause of the Fourteenth Amendment with any substantive content. When they were first asked to do so, they declined, noting that the regulation of slaughterhouses in New Orleans did not constitute the sort of "deprivation of property within the meaning of that provision."[28] In a series of cases from 1873 to 1890, the Court continued to deny that any doctrine of substantive due process could be derived from the Constitution.[29] But there were ominous stirrings. As the personnel of the Court

25. Ibid., 430 (Justice Selden), 453 (Justice Hubbard).
26. 60 U.S. (19 Howard) 393 (1857).
27. Ibid., 450.
28. *The Slaughter-House Cases*, 83 U.S. 36 (1873), 81. Justice Miller insisted that to hold otherwise would have the unhappy effect of constituting the Supreme Court as a "perpetual censor" of all the legislation of the states.
29. *Munn v. Illinois*, 94 U.S. 113 (1877); *Davidson v. New Orleans*, 96 U.S. 97 (1878); *Stone v. Farmers' Loan and Trust Co.*, 116 U.S. 307 (1886).

was changing, there was an emerging willingness on the part of some justices to see more in the due process clause.[30]

Just how far those new inclinations extended was made clear in *Chicago, Milwaukee, and St. Paul Railway Co. v. Minnesota* when the Court for the first time invalidated the rates set by a state regulatory commission as a deprivation of property without due process of law.[31] Then four years later the Court asserted its power to declare the enactments of state legislatures invalid because of the due process clause;[32] in another four years they actually did so.[33] By 1896, Justice Rufus Peckham made clear how secure the revolution in the due process of law had become. "The liberty mentioned in the [Fourteenth] Amendment means, not only the right of the citizen to be free from the mere physical restraint of his person, as by incarceration, but the term is deemed to embrace the right of the citizen to be free in the enjoyment of all his faculties."[34]

The doctrine of substantive due process came into full flower in 1905 with *Lochner v. New York*.[35] The standard for constitutional adjudication under the due process clause was now whether the law in question was "a fair, reasonable, and appropriate exercise of the police power of the state, or [. . .] an unreasonable, unnecessary, and arbitrary interference with the right of the individual to his personal liberty."[36] The protection of economic liberties under the rubric of "liberty of contract" under the due process clause was finally abandoned only in 1937 in *West Coast Hotel v. Parrish*.[37]

---

30. In 1887 the Court announced they were "under a solemn duty—to look at the substance of things whenever they enter upon the inquiry whether the legislature transcended the limits of its authority." *Mugler v. Kansas*, 123 U.S. 623 (1887), 661.

31. 134 U.S. 418 (1890).

32. *Reagan v. Farmers' Loan and Trust Co.*, 154 U.S. 362 (1894).

33. *Smyth v. Ames*, 169 U.S. 466 (1898).

34. *Allgeyer v. Louisiana*, 165 U.S. 578 (1897).

35. 198 U.S. 45 (1905).

36. Ibid., 56.

37. 300 U.S. 379 (1937).

Between *Lochner* and *West Coast Hotel*, the Court used the doctrine of substantive due process to invalidate laws that ranged from
providing minimum wages for women to prohibiting the teaching
of foreign languages to denying parents the right to send their children to parochial schools.[38] Along the way, seemingly just for good
measure, the Court also announced that the Fourteenth Amendment
could be used to apply the First Amendment to the states.[39] In each
case, the Court had openly engaged in the "loose and unhistorical
. . . interpretation" that was seen to be such a danger when the
justices had first begun their construction of the idea that due process of law was not merely a procedural concern but had a substantive core that allowed judges to invalidate legislation.[40] Although
the Court in *West Coast Hotel* declined to invalidate a state law
under the doctrine of substantive due process, it also pointedly
refused to annihilate the doctrine itself, leaving it to return another
day.[41]

In many ways 1937 would prove fundamentally important for
the foundation of a right to privacy whose establishment was nearly
thirty years in the future. In two decisions that year the Supreme
Court established new doctrines that eventually served to allow the
judicial creativity of *Griswold v. Connecticut* (1965). The first was

38. *Adkins v. Children's Hospital*, 261 U.S. 525 (1923); *Meyer v. Nebraska*, 262
U.S. 390 (1923); *Pierce v. Society of Sisters*, 268 U.S. 510 (1925).
39. *Gitlow v. New York*, 268 U.S. 652 (1925). For a critique of *Gitlow* and a
warning of the dangers of the opinion, see Charles Warren, "The New 'Liberty' under
the Fourteenth Amendment," *Harvard Law Review* 39 (1926): 431.
40. For a thorough review of the rise of the doctrine of substantive due process
see Raoul Berger, *Government by Judiciary* (Cambridge: Harvard University Press,
1977), 249–282. See also Christopher Wolfe, *The Rise of Modern Judicial Review:
From Constitutional Interpretation to Judge-Made Law* (New York: Basic Books,
1986), 144–163; and Eugene W. Hickok Jr. and Gary L. McDowell, *Justice vs. Law:
Courts and Politics in American Society* (New York: Free Press, 1993), 80–121.
41. "Liberty under the Constitution," Chief Justice Hughes wrote, "is . . . necessarily subject to the restraints of due process, and regulation which is reasonable in
relation to its subject and is adopted in the interests of the community is due process."
300 U.S. 379, 391.

Palko v. Connecticut in which Justice Benjamin Cardozo addressed the question whether the due process clause of the Fourteenth Amendment incorporated the Bill of Rights and made those provisions applicable to the states.[42] In Cardozo's view, all the provisions of the Bill of Rights were not created equal. Only those that were "of the very essence of a scheme of ordered liberty" should be applied to the states through the due process clause.[43] The test, said Cardozo, was whether the rights in question were those "implicit in the concept of ordered liberty" and "so rooted in the traditions and conscience of our people as to be ranked fundamental."[44] As a general matter, those more procedural rights (such as the protection against double jeopardy, the issue in the case at hand) were not equal to such rights as "freedom of thought and speech"—rights Cardozo insisted formed "the matrix, the indispensable condition of nearly every other form of freedom."[45] The two main contributions of *Palko* were, first, the idea that all rights are not equal, that there is a hierarchy; and second, that it is up to the justices to determine which rights are fundamental and apply to the states and which ones are not. The old substantive due process standard of "reasonableness" was left alive and well.

The second case of 1937 that contributed to the creation and expansion of a constitutional right to privacy was *Carolene Products Co. v. United States*.[46] The issue in the case—the power of Congress to prohibit the interstate transportation of filled milk—is of no interest to the debate over rights or privacy. What makes the

---

42. The Marshall Court had denied that the Bill of Rights applied to the states in *Barron v. Baltimore*, 7 Peters 243 (1833), but most recently the Court had ruled that the Fourteenth Amendment could serve to alter that relationship in *Gitlow v. New York*, 268 U.S. 652 (1925).

43. 302 U.S. 319 (1937), 325.

44. Ibid.; ibid. Quoting himself from the majority opinion in *Snyder v. Massachusetts*, 291 U.S. 97, 105.

45. 302 U.S. 319, 327.

46. 304 U.S. 144 (1937).

case significant is the *obiter dictum* of Justice Harlan Fiske Stone that was embedded in a mere footnote to the opinion. Confirming that the Court was now willing to defer to the Congress on the propriety of economic and business regulation, it was not quite so willing when it came to personal liberties. In particular, he warned, if legislation is found by the Court to suggest a "prejudice against discrete and insular minorities," then such legislation can expect a "more searching judicial inquiry."[47] This new approach to due process of law as dealing with personal rather than property rights would still have at its core the problem of judicial arbitrariness as the justices sought to measure the "reasonableness" of the law.

These new doctrinal strands of the Court's thinking came together with an institutional vengeance in the privacy cases. The issue that became the point of *Griswold v. Connecticut* had come to the Court before in *Poe v. Ullman*, but the Court had declined to reach the merits of the case.[48] Yet in the dissent of Justice John Marshall Harlan, it was clear that the doctrine of substantive due process was still lurking just around the doctrinal corner. As he insisted, "the full scope of the liberty guaranteed by the Due Process Clause cannot be found in or limited by the precise terms of the specific guarantees elsewhere provided in the Constitution. This 'liberty' is not a series of isolated points . . . [but] is a rational continuum which, broadly speaking, includes a freedom from all substantial arbitrary impositions and purposeless restraints."[49] The split among the justices on this question was clearly revealed two years later—and two years before *Griswold*—in *Ferguson v. Skrupa* (1963). In that decision for a unanimous Court, Justice Hugo Black wrote that "[t]here was a time when the Due Process Clause was used by this Court to strike down laws which were thought unreasonable, that is, unwise or incompatible with some

47. Ibid., 152, n. 4.
48. 367 U.S. 497 (1961).
49. Ibid., 543.

particular economic or social philosophy." But that time had passed. "The doctrine . . . that due process authorizes courts to hold laws unconstitutional when they believe the legislature has acted unwisely has long since been discarded. We have returned to the original constitutional proposition that courts do not substitute their social and economic beliefs for the judgment of legislative bodies, who are elected to pass laws."[50] Thus was the state of doctrinal confusion when the issues in *Poe* came back to the Court for resolution in *Griswold*.

In *Griswold v. Connecticut* the Supreme Court ruled that a Connecticut statute making the use of birth control measures by married couples illegal was a violation of "a right of privacy older than the Bill of Rights—older than our political parties, older than our school system."[51] The problem for the Court was that the law obviously violated no particular provision of the Constitution. It perhaps would not have been surprising if Justice William O. Douglas had rested his majority opinion on the discredited but not completely dead idea of substantive due process, such as in *Lochner v. New York*;[52] but he explicitly chose to "decline that invitation."[53] Instead of exhuming a doctrine many thought best left buried (and since he had joined Black's opinion in *Ferguson* two years earlier), Douglas held that the Connecticut law had run afoul of "penumbral rights" that were, in his view, "formed by emanations" from "specific guarantees in the Bill of Rights."[54] This sweeping opinion had been forewarned by Douglas in his dissent in *Poe*. There he had made clear that in his view "'due process' as used in the Fourteenth Amendment includes all of the first eight Amendments . . . [but is not] restricted and confined to them." The idea of "[l]iberty is a

50. 372 U.S. 726 (1963), 729, 730.
51. 381 U.S. 479 (1965); ibid., 486.
52. 198 U.S. 45 (1905).
53. 381 U.S. 479, 482.
54. Ibid., 484.

conception that sometimes gains content from the emanations of other specific guarantees."[55] By any measure, this was judicial creativity of unequaled boldness.

Following *Griswold*, the Court found that those penumbras were capacious enough constitutionally to protect the right of unmarried couples to use birth control and the right to abortion.[56] Because of the foundation of the right to privacy and the understanding of judicial power that had allowed the Court to create it,[57] there was never any reason to think that in any meaningful way it had reached "the limit of its logic" with the abortion decision,

55. 367 U.S. 497, 516–517.

56. *Eisenstadt v. Baird*, 405 U.S. 438 (1972); *Roe v. Wade*, 410 U.S. 113 (1973).

57. There is no doubt that the justices involved in the drafting of the decision in *Griswold* knew that what they were doing was creating a new constitutional right. On April 24, 1965, Justice William Brennan wrote to Justice William O. Douglas with suggestions for improving the draft opinion Justice Douglas had sent to him. Douglas had initially been seeking the right of marital privacy in the notion of the freedom of association, a right earlier created by the Court by blending the rights of freedom of speech and freedom of assembly that are textually present in the First Amendment. Brennan cautioned against this approach. While insisting that Douglas was right in rejecting any approach based on the old doctrine of substantive due process, Brennan counseled that the best approach would be to follow the Court's earlier example "in *creating* a right of association . . . [from] the First Amendment to protect something not literally within its terminology of speech and assembly, because the interest protected is so closely related to speech and assembly." As he saw it, such a tack was far better: "Instead of expanding the First Amendment right of association to include marriage, why not say that what has been done for the First Amendment can also be done for some of the other fundamental guarantees of the Bill of Rights?" Brennan's goal was to see "a right to privacy *created* out of the Fourth Amendment and the self-incrimination clause of the Fifth, together with the Third, in much the same way as the right to associate has been *created* out of the First." Such a ploy would allow the Court to "hurdle" the "obstacle" posed by the fact that "the association of husband and wife is not mentioned in the Bill of Rights" and thus "effect a reversal in this case." William J. Brennan to William O. Douglas, April 24, 1965, Manuscript Division, Library of Congress. Emphasis supplied.

For a glimpse of the law office politics of the justices' chambers as they wrestled with what to do about the opinions in *Griswold*, see David J. Garrow, *Liberty and Sexuality: The Right to Privacy and the Making of Roe v. Wade* (New York: Macmillan, 1994), 229–260.

however politically tumultuous that case would prove to be.[58] Even more important to the idea of the right to privacy and its expansion than *Roe v. Wade* and the cases that came in its wake was the decision of the Court upholding *Roe* in *Planned Parenthood of Southeastern Pennsylvania v. Casey*. For there the justices made it very clear how truly limitless was the idea of "liberty" and how great was their own self-proclaimed power to shape it as they pleased, regardless of what the representative institutions of the federal and state governments might think.

The plurality opinion of Justices Kennedy, O'Connor, and Souter in *Casey* went far beyond merely upholding *Roe*. It undertook to establish an understanding of judicial power and constitutional interpretation far more radical than what any earlier court had ever suggested. It was not enough merely to embrace as they did the intellectually rickety structure of substantive due process by noting once again that "a literal reading of the [Due Process] Clause might suggest that it governs only procedures by which a State may deprive persons of liberty." Such a literal reading would miss the essence of modern notions of judicial power. Indeed, "for at least 105 years, at least since *Mugler v. Kansas* . . . the Clause has been understood to contain a substantive component as well."[59] And the "outer limits of that substantive sphere of liberty" were defined by neither "the Bill of Rights nor the specific practices of States at the time of the adoption of the Fourteenth Amendment."[60] The fact was, the boundaries of the due process clause were "not susceptible

---

58. Benjamin N. Cardozo, *The Nature of the Judicial Process* (New Haven, Conn.: Yale University Press, 1921), 51.

In his dissent in *Lawrence v. Texas*, Justice Scalia insisted that "[s]tate laws against bigamy, same-sex marriage, adult incest, prostitution, masturbation, adultery, fornication, bestiality, and obscenity" would be subject to invalidation since the Court had now overruled its earlier opinion in *Bowers v. Hardwick* that states have the right to pass laws "based on moral choices." 156 L. Ed. 2d., 533.

59. 505 U.S. 833 (1992), 846.

60. Ibid., 848.

of expression as a simple rule." That substantive component of "liberty" depended on nothing besides the "reasoned judgment" of the Court itself.[61]

What was most shocking about the Kennedy, O'Connor, and Souter opinion in *Casey* was the utter disdain it reflected for the idea of popular government. The Court was not simply intended, as Alexander Hamilton said in *The Federalist*, to be an "intermediate" institution between the people and their government "in order, among other things, to keep the latter within the limits assigned to their authority."[62] It was something far more. Indeed, the essence of judicial power as presented in *Casey* was that of an institution "invested with the authority to . . . speak before all others for [the people's] constitutional ideals."[63] The power of the Court to declare such values—and the people's willingness to acquiesce in those declarations—was to Kennedy, O'Connor, and Souter what gave legitimacy to the people as "a nation dedicated to the rule of law."[64] It was precisely this view of its own power to "speak before all others" for the constitutional ideals of the people that would in time bring the Court to the point of overruling *Bowers v. Hardwick* (1986) in order to expand ever further the "outer limits of the substantive sphere of liberty" in *Lawrence v. Texas.*

The underlying reason that the Court in *Lawrence* could so easily overrule *Bowers v. Hardwick* in order to extend the "outer limits" of privacy to include homosexual sodomy was that *Bowers* itself rested on the same substantive due process foundation that *Griswold* and its ancestors and heirs shared. Justice Byron White's majority opinion upholding the power of the states to prohibit homosexuality as a matter of moral choice, viewing it as "immoral

---

61. Ibid., 849.
62. Jacob E. Cooke, ed., *The Federalist* (Middletown, Conn.: Wesleyan University Press, 1961), No. 78, 525.
63. 505 U.S. 833, 868.
64. Ibid., 865.

and unacceptable," did not rest on the fact that the Constitution was silent on such matters, thus leaving them to the states.[65] Instead, the state statute was valid because such moral prohibitions had "ancient roots."[66] As in *Griswold*, so also in *Bowers*: such rights rest on nothing firmer or more certain than that the Court found them to be "so rooted in the traditions and conscience of our people as to be ranked fundamental."[67] All Justice Kennedy had to do in *Lawrence* was to show that Justice White's history in *Bowers* was, at the very least, "not without doubt."[68] It certainly was not enough to sustain the "substantive validity" of the law in question.[69] Justice Kennedy's history, he insisted, displayed "an emerging awareness that liberty gives substantial protection to adult persons in deciding how to conduct their private lives in matters pertaining to sex."[70] The "ethical and moral principles" that were deeply enough felt by the people of Texas to pass the law at hand were no match for the justices' confidence in their "own moral code."[71] Such is the judicial advantage of an unwritten constitution of evolving meaning over a written one with fixed meaning.

The Political Price of Privacy

From the beginning of the Court's infatuation with an implicit right to privacy there had been an older tradition of thinking about courts

65. 478 U.S. 186, 196.

66. Ibid., 192. Having accepted the line of substantive due process cases as precedent, Justice White tried to draw a line: "Nor are we inclined to take a more expansive view of our authority to discover new fundamental rights imbedded in the Due Process Clause. The Court is most vulnerable and comes nearest to illegitimacy when it deals with judge-made constitutional law having little or no cognizable roots in the language or design of the Constitution." Ibid., 194.

67. *Palko v. Connecticut*, 302 U.S. 319, 324–325.

68. 156 L. Ed. 2d., 521.

69. Ibid., 523.

70. Ibid., 521.

71. Ibid.

and constitutions, a tradition that stood in opposition to the likes of Justices Douglas and Kennedy. This tradition found expression in dissent throughout the judicial creation of the right to privacy, beginning in *Griswold* itself when Justice Black indicted the Court's resurrection of the doctrine of substantive due process "based on subjective considerations of 'natural justice'" in order to strike down the Connecticut law as simply unacceptable.[72] It is not the duty of the Supreme Court, he insisted, "to keep the Constitution in tune with the times."[73] The framers knew there would be need for change and had provided for it through the formal process of amendment. Although he could agree with Justice Potter Stewart's characterization of the law as "uncommonly silly,"[74] that was not grounds enough for the Court to invalidate it.

Similarly in *Roe v. Wade*, Justice White derided what the Court had done in expanding the right to privacy as nothing more than "an exercise of raw judicial power . . . an improvident and extravagant exercise of the power of judicial review that the Constitution extends to this Court."[75] And to Justice William Rehnquist, the majority decision was more a matter of "judicial legislation than it [was] of a determination of the intent of the drafters of the Fourteenth Amendment." It was, Rehnquist said, "closely attuned" to the opinion of Justice Peckham in *Lochner v. New York*.[76]

When it came to the *Casey* decision upholding *Roe*, Justice Antonin Scalia considered the claim in the opinion by Kennedy, O'Connor, and Souter that it fell to the Court to speak "before all others" for the fundamental constitutional ideals of the people—to be nothing less than a "Nietzschean vision" that had no place in constitutional law.[77] Indeed, the decision went beyond even the old

72. 381 U.S. 479, 522.
73. Ibid., 521.
74. Ibid., 527.
75. *Doe v. Bolton*, 410 U.S. 179 (1973), 222.
76. 410 U.S. 113, 174.
77. 505 U.S. 833, 996.

line of substantive due process cases. The result was "a new mode of constitutional adjudication that relies not upon text and traditional practice to determine the law, but upon what the Court calls 'reasoned judgment' . . . which turns out to be nothing but philosophical predilection and moral intuition."[78] To Scalia, the lesson of *Casey* was simple: "The Imperial Judiciary lives."[79]

In both *Casey* and *Lawrence*, Justice Scalia emphasized that what is at stake when the Court is "impatient of democratic change" and undertakes to create new constitutional rights is the right of the people to constitutional self-government.[80] If, as Justice Kennedy insisted, "later generations can see that laws once thought necessary and proper in fact serve only to oppress," then "later generations can repeal those laws." In Scalia's view (a view shared by Rehnquist and Clarence Thomas), "it is the premise of our system that those judgments are to be made by the people, and not imposed by a governing caste that knows best."[81] One need not agree with the moral choices made by the people of a state about abortion or homosexuality to recognize the innate right of the people under the Constitution to make those choices free from judicial intervention based on a contrived constitutional right. As he would put it elsewhere, "[i]t is simply not compatible with democratic theory that laws mean whatever they ought to mean, and that unelected judges should decide what that is."[82]

This dissenting tradition from Justice Black to Justice Scalia has roots deep in the constitutional history of the United States, and even beyond.[83] One of the earliest and most famous refutations

78. Ibid., 1000.
79. Ibid., 996.
80. 156 L. Ed. 2d, 542.
81. Ibid.
82. Antonin Scalia, *A Matter of Interpretation: Federal Courts and the Law* (Princeton, N.J.: Princeton University Press, 1997), 22.
83. See Raoul Berger, "'Original Intention' in Historical Perspective," *George Washington Law Review* 54 (1986): 296.

of the idea that judges could recur to fundamental principles or natural law in reaching their decisions came from Justice James Iredell against Justice Samuel Chase's claim in *Calder v. Bull* in 1798. "If . . . the legislature . . . shall pass a law within the general scope of their constitutional powers," he wrote, "the court cannot pronounce it void, merely because it is, in their judgment, contrary to the principles of natural justice." The reason was plain: "The ideas of natural justice are regulated by no fixed standard: the ablest and the purest men have differed upon the subject; and all that the court could properly say, in such an event, would be that the legislature possessed of an equal right of opinion, had passed an act which in the opinion of the judges, was inconsistent with the abstract principles of natural justice."[84]

Similarly, both Chief Justice John Marshall and Justice Joseph Story, despite their rare and insignificant flirtations with a realm of rights beyond the textual Constitution, were committed to the idea of the positive law of the Constitution and its representative institutions. For Marshall, the very idea of a written constitution was "the greatest improvement on political institutions." It was the embodiment of the people's "original right to establish, for their future government, such principles as, in their opinion, shall most conduce to their own happiness." Those principles once established in a constitution "are deemed fundamental . . . [and] are designed to be permanent."[85] It was not empty rhetoric when he later exhorted his fellow justices to "never forget that it is a *constitution* we are expounding."[86] And when the argument was made before the Court that the provisions of the first ten amendments to the Constitution applied to the states, Marshall rejected that claim, noting that "[h]ad the framers of these amendments intended them to be limitations on the powers of the state governments, they would

---

84. 3 U.S. (3 Dall.) 386, 398–399.
85. *Marbury v. Madison*, 5 U.S. (1 Cranch) 137 (1803), 176, 178.
86. *McCulloch v. Maryland*, 17 U.S. (Wheaton) 316 (1819), 407.

have imitated the framers of the original constitution, and have expressed that intention . . . in plain and intelligible language." Without that expressed intention, the Court could not so apply them.[87] For Marshall, no matter how alluring might be the principles of natural justice, there was no doubt that "*intention* is the most sacred rule of interpretation" and that "the great duty of a judge who construes an instrument is to find the intention of its makers."[88]

Justice Story was equally clear on these matters. "The first and fundamental rule in the interpretation of all instruments," he said in introducing his chapter "Rules of Interpretation" in his *Commentaries on the Constitution of the United States*, "is to construe them according to the sense of the terms and the intention of the parties."[89] Any judicial departure from the "true import and sense of [the Constitution's] powers" would be a "usurping of the functions of a legislator, and deserting those of an expounder of the law."[90] In Story's view, the Constitution was to have "a fixed, uniform, permanent construction. It should be . . . not dependent upon the passions or parties of particular times, but the same yesterday, to-day, and forever."[91] And should a Court undertake to be guided by "the rights . . . arising from natural law and justice," this undertaking would prove "the most formidable instrument of arbitrary power that could well be devised."[92] Story understood constitutions as "instruments of a practical nature"; when it came to interpreting them, he did not think they were "designed for met-

---

87. *Barron v. Baltimore*, 32 U.S. (7 Peters) 243 (1833), 250.
88. Gerald Gunther, ed., *John Marshall's Defense of* McCulloch v. Maryland (Stanford, Calif.: Stanford University Press, 1969), 167, 168–169.
89. Joseph Story, *Commentaries on the Constitution of the United States*, 4th ed., 2 vols. (Boston: Little, Brown and Co., 1873), I: 295.
90. Ibid., 314–315.
91. Ibid., 315.
92. Joseph Story, *Commentaries on Equity Jurisprudence*, 12th ed., 2 vols. (Boston: Little, Brown and Co., 1877), I: 15.

aphysical or logical subtleties, for niceties of expression, for critical propriety, for elaborate shades of meaning, or for the exercise of philosophical acuteness or judicial research." The language was to be "expounded in its plain, obvious, and common sense"; there was no place for "any recondite meaning or extraordinary gloss."[93]

This same understanding constituted the foundation of Justice Benjamin Curtis's dissent to Chief Justice Taney's opinion in *Dred Scott*. Although Taney insisted that his opinion was based on the original meaning and intention of the Constitution "when it came from the hands of its framers and was voted on and adopted by the people of the United States,"[94] Justice Curtis thought otherwise. He knew Taney's effort to be a blatant and intentional misconstruction of the Constitution "upon reasons purely political."[95] In Curtis's view, "when a strict interpretation of the Constitution, according to the fixed rules which govern the interpretation of laws is abandoned, and the theoretical opinions of individuals are allowed to control its meaning, we have no longer a Constitution; we are under the government of individual men, who for the time being have power to declare what the Constitution is, according to their own views of what it ought to mean."[96] Such an interpretation means the demise of "republican government."[97]

It was this question of the legitimate bounds of republican government under a federal constitution that also concerned Justice Oliver Wendell Holmes over the course of the first era of substantive due process, at least when it came to striking down economic legislation. He had grave and nagging doubts about the "vague contours" of the idea of substantive due process as the grounds for invalidating statutes rather than explicit constitutional provisions.[98]

93. Story, *Commentaries on the Constitution*, I: 322.
94. 60 U.S. (19 Howard) 393, 426.
95. Ibid., 621.
96. Ibid.
97. Ibid.
98. *Adkins v. Children's Hospital of the District of Columbia*, 261 U.S. 525, 568.

He saw danger in "the ever increasing scope given to the Fourteenth Amendment in cutting down . . . the constitutional rights of
the states." He could not believe, he said, that "the amendment was
intended to give [the Court] *carte blanche* to embody [the justices']
economic and moral beliefs in its prohibitions." As things stood, it
seemed to Holmes that the sky was the limit to what the Court
might choose to do.[99]

Conclusion

Constitutional self-government is not possible if the Supreme Court
of the United States assumes—and is allowed to assume—the
power to declare invalid, based on the right to privacy, the state
laws that seek to express moral choices. That the Court has undertaken to do this because of the notion of substantive due process
is the bad news. But it is not the worst news. Far more troubling
is the fact that there is not now on the Court any justice willing to
repudiate the idea that the due process clauses do not deal simply
with procedures but reach to the "substantive validity" of the laws.

To his credit, Justice White in his opinion in *Bowers* was at
least willing to cast doubt on the prudence of those precedents—
albeit stopping far short of rejecting them as a matter of principle.
The willingness of earlier courts, he suggested, to assume that the
due process clauses have a "substantive content . . . recognizing
rights that have little or no textual support in the constitutional
language" had posed problems in the past. But while "much of the
substantive gloss" had been repudiated, there was much that
remained. Thus he was willing to resist the call to find the right of
homosexual sodomy included in the meaning of liberty in those
clauses. "The Court," he pointed out, "is most vulnerable and
comes nearest to illegitimacy when it deals with judge-made con-

99. *Baldwin v. Missouri*, 281 U.S. 586 (1930), 595.

stitutional law having little or no cognizable roots in the language or design of the Constitution."[100]

Today Justice Scalia is willing to condemn the idea of substantive due process but most explicitly only outside the pages of the *United States Reports*.[101] In views expressed off the bench, he has argued forcefully that the "inescapable terms" of the due process clauses guarantee "only process." The result of the line of cases creating and perpetuating the idea of substantive due process has been "to render democratically adopted texts mere springboards for judicial lawmaking."[102] But the weight of the precedents is such that even he tends to acquiesce in their lingering legitimacy as a matter of binding constitutional law. The only question is how to prevent expanding the doctrine to include new judge-made rights that might satisfy his colleagues' yearning for social justice.[103]

---

100. 478 U.S. 186, 191, 194. Justice White here was repeating part of his dissent in *Moore v. East Cleveland*, 431 U.S. 494 (1977), 544. He there went on to argue that "the present construction of the Due Process Clause represents a major judicial gloss on its terms, as well as on the anticipation of the Framers." As a result, he warned, "the Court should be extremely reluctant to breathe still further substantive content into the Due Process Clause so as to strike down legislation adopted by a State or city to promote its welfare." Ibid.

101. Justice Scalia has come closest to denouncing the doctrine in a series of cases dealing with punitive damages wherein he has raised fundamental questions about the idea of substantive due process. See *Pacific Mutual Life Insurance Co. v. Haslip*, 499 U.S. 1 (1991), 24–39; *TXO Production Corp. v. Alliance Resources*, 509 U.S. 443 (1993), 470–472; *BMW of North America v. Gore* 517 U.S. 559 (1996), 598–607. He has also extended his criticism to criminal procedure in *Albright v. Oliver*, 510 U.S. 266 (1994), 275–276. In *Albright* (p. 275) he insisted that while the due process clause may be understood to incorporate "certain explicit substantive protections of the Bill of Rights," it was not home to other "(unspecified) liberties." He had been even more explicit in *TXO Production Corp.* (pp. 470–471) where he argued that he was unwilling to "accept the proposition that [the due process clause] is the secret repository of all sorts of other, unenumerated rights—however fashionable that proposition may have been . . . at the time of the *Lochner*-era cases. . . ."

102. Scalia, *Matter of Interpretation*, 24–25.

103. See, for example, his opinion in *Michael H. v. Gerald D.* in which he conceded that substantive due process "is an established part of our constitutional jurisprudence" but sought to fence it in by recourse to history and tradition, relying on Cardozo's

The claims of precedent in a common law system are compelling; they are less so as a matter of constitutional law. To allow previously and wrongly decided cases to alter in perpetuity the original meaning of the Constitution is to misunderstand the nature of constitutional government and inevitably to supplant the founders' intentions with contemporary judges' personal notions of justice. A strict and unyielding adherence to precedent would allow nothing to be done about what has been called "the derelicts of constitutional law," universally abhorred errors of judicial lawmaking such as *Dred Scott* v. *Sandford* and *Plessy* v. *Ferguson*.[104] Although Justices Kennedy, O'Connor, and Souter in *Casey* might be willing to defend such a strict embrace of *stare decisis* as essential to maintaining the Court's legitimacy, one is reminded of a more sober view of the doctrine, that "precedents prove only what was done, and not what was well done."[105] That is most assuredly the case when it comes to the misbegotten string of cases imposing the notion of substantive due process.

Unless a repudiation of the doctrine takes place, and it is expunged as unconstitutional from the body of the nation's constitutional law—and that is likely to take place only by a constitutional amendment emphasizing that due process of law is a procedural, not a substantive, concern—government by the judiciary will continue and with it the further erosion of constitutional self-government in any meaningful sense. Indeed, it is impossible to avoid the conclusion that the species of judicial activism in the right to privacy cases is inconsistent not only with the origin, his-

---

standard of protections "so rooted in the traditions and conscience of our people as to be ranked fundamental." 491 U.S. 110 (1989), 121, 122.

104. 60 U.S. (19 How.) 393 (1857); 163 U.S. 537 (1896). Philip B. Kurland, *Politics, the Constitution, and the Warren Court* (Chicago: University of Chicago Press, 1970), 186.

105. Thomas Hobbes, *A Dialogue between a Philosopher and a Student of the Common Laws of England*, ed. Joseph Cropsey (Chicago: University of Chicago Press, 1971), 129.

tory, and meaning of the Constitution but with the understanding of popular government in its most fundamental sense. And, as history shows, there is no reason to think that the expansion of this judicially created right has reached its limits.

There is, in fact, every reason to believe, as Justice Scalia warned in his dissent in *Lawrence*, that there will be few laws that allegedly impinge on the notion of privacy that will be found constitutional in the years ahead. Indeed, since *Bowers* v. *Hardwick* was overruled on the ground that the states do not have the legitimate authority to pass laws "based on moral choices" when it comes to sexual intimacy, it is hard to see how "[s]tate laws against bigamy, same-sex marriage, adult incest, prostitution, masturbation, adultery, fornication, bestiality, and obscenity" could ever pass constitutional muster.[106] Justice Kennedy's choice of words in his opinion in *Lawrence* seems to make that clear. Under the substantive due process logic of Kennedy's opinion, liberty "presumes an autonomy of self that includes . . . certain intimate contact."[107] Precisely what sort of "intimate contact" is included will depend not on constitutional text or intention or even the legal history and traditions of the country; it will depend only on what a majority of the justices conclude is "reasonable."

At the height of the controversies over judge-made law in the 1930s, it was lamented that "[u]nder the guise of the supremacy of the law, we have established the supremacy of the judges."[108] As *Lawrence v. Texas* makes clear, nothing has changed.

106. 156 L. Ed. 2d., 533.
107. Ibid., 515.
108. J. A. C. Grant, "The Natural Law Background of Due Process," *Columbia Law Review* 31 (1931): 56, 81.

3

A Court
Tilting against
Religious Liberty

Terry Eastland

The First Amendment provides in part, "Congress shall make no law respecting an establishment of religion or prohibiting the free exercise thereof." The amendment became part of the Constitution in 1791, but not until 1940, in *Cantwell v. Connecticut*, did the Supreme Court declare that the states are "as incompetent as Congress to enact" laws establishing religion or prohibiting its free exercise.[1] Citing the Fourteenth Amendment's provision that no state may deprive a person of liberty without due process of law, the Court held that "this fundamental concept of liberty . . . embraces the liberties guaranteed by the First Amendment." Before *Cantwell*, the states had passed plenty of laws touching on religion—far more than Congress. *Cantwell* meant that state laws involving religion could be challenged under the First Amendment. With the necessary plaintiffs quickly emerging, the Court has now decided a long list of cases concerning a wide range of issues, most of them arising from the states.

---

1. 310 U.S. 296 (1940).

The Court's religion jurisprudence is almost entirely a product of the cases since *Cantwell*. Legal scholars agree that it is an intellectual mess. Unfortunately, that is not the worst that can be said about it. The truth is that the Court's religion decisions have done serious damage to the country.

Religious liberty is a core American value. Indeed, some scholars call it our "first liberty." The purpose of the treatment of religion in the First Amendment was to protect religious liberty. Yet rather than understanding the First Amendment as containing a single clause with that purpose, the Court has persisted in finding two religion clauses in the amendment—the establishment clause and the free exercise clause—and in reading them independently of one another. Through the establishment clause the Court has insisted on a stricter "separation of church and state" than the original intent of the First Amendment demands. The Court has used the clause to push religion from the public schools and to inhibit efforts to provide public aid for church-related schools. Meanwhile, the Court has had little to say about "free exercise" and in recent years has treated it as a subset of free speech, lacking any independent value. Thanks to the Court, Americans are not as free to exercise religion as the Constitution, properly interpreted, allows.

The Court is a major reason that the country today is far more secular than the one a dwindling number of Americans grew up in. The secularizing influence of the Court's decisions can be seen in many areas, not least our public schools.

Early Cases

In *Minersville (Pa.) School District v. Gobitis* (1940), public school authorities required students to salute and pledge allegiance to the flag as part of a daily exercise.[2] Two students, both Jehovah's

2. 310 U.S. 586 (1940).

Witnesses, refused to participate on the ground of religious conscience. For them, saluting the flag "of any earthly government" was idolatrous. The students were expelled. Their father, Walter Gobitis, filed a lawsuit alleging a violation of "free exercise." Gobitis won in the lower courts, but the Supreme Court ruled in favor of the school district, holding that the First Amendment did not exempt the students from the compulsory exercise.

Citing the decision in *Gobitis*, the West Virginia State Board of Education voted to require all public school students to participate in a flag-salute ceremony. Expulsion was the penalty for anyone who refused, and the parents of children so expelled were subject to criminal prosecution. Once again students who were Jehovah's Witnesses objected on the ground of religious conscience. But in deciding *West Virginia State Board of Education v. Barnette* (1943), the Court took the broader First Amendment position that no one should be forced to salute and pledge allegiance to the flag.[3] At stake, wrote Justice Robert Jackson, was "the constitutional liberty of the individual."

Neither *Gobitis* nor *Barnette* concerned the First Amendment's ban on establishing religion. But soon enough the Court had before it a case—*Everson v. Board of Education* (1947)—in which it would, for the first time, declare the meaning of that provision.[4] Between 1937 and 1941 the New Jersey legislature debated whether the state, which had a substantial Catholic population, should fund the transportation costs of parochial school students. In 1941 the state passed a law authorizing local school boards to make rules and contracts for transporting children "to and from school other than a public school." Ewing Township, like other jurisdictions, proceeded to implement the law. Previously it had reimbursed the fares paid to public carriers by parents of students

3. 319 U.S. 624 (1943).
4. 330 U.S. 1 (1947).

attending public schools. Now it decided to reimburse as well the fares paid by the parents of students going to parochial schools.

Arch Everson, a resident of Ewing Township and executive director of the New Jersey Taxpayers Association, sued the state. As it happened, Everson was a nominal plaintiff. The lawsuit was initiated and paid for by the Junior Order of United American Mechanics. The JOUAM was a century-old organization with a nativist, anti-Catholic past. It was a vigorous supporter of public schools, including their lingering Protestant orientation. A leading opponent of the parochial school bus bill, the JOUAM was now continuing the same battle in the courts.

Everson and his allies succeeded in persuading the Court to interpret the establishment clause as Thomas Jefferson had said the First Amendment should be interpreted—as mandating a "wall of separation between church & State." In his opinion for the Court, Justice Hugo Black spelled out what this "wall of separation" meant—among other things, that no government can pass laws which "aid all religions" and that "no tax in any amount, large or small, can be levied to support any religious activities or institutions, whatever they may be called, or whatever form they may adopt to teach or practice religion." Surely, on those terms, New Jersey had violated the clause. But Black reached the opposite conclusion by maintaining that the transportation subsidy benefited not the parochial schools themselves but the children attending them.

The four dissenting justices, all of whom voted to strike down the reimbursement scheme, were incredulous. "The undertones of the opinion, advocating complete and uncompromising separation of Church from State," wrote Justice Robert Jackson in dissent, "seem utterly discordant with its conclusion yielding support to their commingling in educational matters. The case which irresistibly comes to mind as the most fitting precedent is that of Julia who, according to Byron's reports, 'whispering "I will ne'er consent,"—consented.'" In a case decided sixteen years later, *Abington v. Schempp* (1963), Justice William O. Douglas, a member of Black's majority, confessed to a change of mind about *Everson*.[5] Had Douglas voted as he later came to believe he should have, a majority would have found the bus subsidy unconstitutional.

Everson's importance lay less in the result, which happened to be correct, than in the separationist doctrine it embraced. Agreed to by all nine justices, the doctrine provided the foundation for many of the religion decisions the Court would hand down over the next several decades. Yet, as some later justices have realized, the doctrine was grounded in dubious history. Thirty-eight years after *Everson*, in *Wallace v. Jaffree* (1985), Justice William Rehnquist carefully examined the actual framing of the establishment clause—a task no justice in *Everson* or since had undertaken—in concluding that it "forbade establishment of a national religion and . . . preference among religious sects or denominations."[6] In pointed disagreement with the justices in *Everson*, Rehnquist added that "the establishment clause did not require government neutrality between religion and irreligion nor did it prohibit the Federal Government from providing nondiscriminatory aid to religion." Rehnquist's withering judgment was this: "There is simply no historical foundation for the proposition that the Framers intended to build the 'wall of separation' that was constitutionalized in *Everson*." Jefferson's letter to the Danbury Baptists did not express the intent of the First Amendment.

It will be noted that in the *Jaffree* case Justice Rehnquist wrote in dissent. The Court has yet to repudiate *Everson*'s wrong history and the wrong doctrine it yielded. Nor has the Court attempted to read the ban on establishing religion in conjunction with the prohibition on free exercise, although the latter is the more fundamental value. Indeed, as political scientist Vincent Phillip Munoz

5. 374 U.S. 203 (1963).
6. 472 U.S. 38 (1985).

has pointed out, Congress in 1791 was prohibited from making an establishment of religion because religious establishments tended to abridge religious liberty.[7]

Religion and the Public Schools

The first schools founded in the colonies had as one of their purposes religious education. The founding generation assumed that religion would be part of education. The Northwest Ordinance, passed in 1787 and then again by the First Congress in 1789, explicitly identified religion as one of the values that schools established in the territory would advance. Public schools, which emerged in the first half of the nineteenth century, retained religious instruction, though less of it was included in the everyday lesson plan as communities became more religiously diverse. During the first decades of the twentieth century, many schools opted for programs in which children were "released" from their classroom schools for an hour during which clergy of their parents' choice would provide religious instruction. Meanwhile, the school day in many parts of the country began with prayer or Bible reading or both.

Everson's separationist doctrine called into question the public schools' various involvements with religion. In *McCollum v. Board of Education* (1948), the Court struck down a released-time program initiated in 1940 in Champaign, Illinois.[8] Teachers from all religious groups choosing to participate were allowed to offer religious instruction in school buildings for one hour once a week. Students in grades four to nine had the option of attending religion classes of their choice (as approved by parents) or continuing their regular studies. The religion teachers weren't paid by the state but

---

7. Vincent Phillip Munoz, "Establishing Free Exercise," *First Things* 138 (December 2003): 14–20.

8. 333 U.S. 203 (1948).

were subject to the approval and supervision of the school super-intendent. Defending itself against Vashti McCollum's contention that the program established religion, the school board argued that the meaning of the establishment clause was not to be found in Jefferson's metaphorical wall of separation. This was a brave argu-ment, since all the Justices who had decided *Everson* only a year earlier still sat on the Court. The argument was rejected, as was the board's actual (and correct) interpretation of the clause—that it forbids only the government's preference of one religion over another, and not impartial government assistance to all religions. Black, again writing for the Court, was unwilling to back away from his *Everson* statement that government may not "aid all relig-ions." A state, he opined, may not "utilize its public school system to aid any or all religious faiths or sects in the dissemination of their doctrines and ideals."

In his recent book, *Separation of Church and State*, University of Chicago law professor Philip Hamburger points out that by the time *Everson* was decided many Protestants had accepted a "Prot-estant" version of separation of church and state. Indeed, Arch Everson had pressed this version of separation in his case, hoping to deny state aid to children attending Catholic schools. *McCollum* stunned Protestants around the country, however, because the stu-dents typically taking advantage of released-time programs were Protestant. Protestants, writes Hamburger, "now suddenly found themselves confronted with a secular version [of separation], which threatened the nonsectarian religiosity of America's public insti-tutions. It was an experience they would feel even more profoundly in the wake of later Supreme Court cases and that would gradually bring many Protestants to recognize that they faced a greater threat from secularism and separation than from Catholicism."[9]

---

9. Philip Hamburger, *Separation of Church and State*, 376–377 (Cambridge: Harvard University Press, 2002).

Zorach v. Clauson (1952) was not one of those later cases.[10]
Here the Court sustained a released-time program from New York
City that differed from the one in *McCollum* in that the religious
instruction it permitted was provided off campus. That fact
impressed Douglas, who in his opinion for the Court said that the
First Amendment does not command a "separation of church and
state" in "all respects." The Court would have to press the concept
to "extremes," he said, to condemn the New York program. And
in that event, the Court would be insisting on a "constitutional
requirement which makes it necessary for government to be hostile
to religion and to throw its weight against efforts to widen the
effective scope of religious influence." Because *McCollum* had
drawn criticism from a wide variety of clergy, Douglas might have
felt compelled to reassure Americans that the Court was not really
hostile to religion. Douglas famously declared, "We are a religious
people whose institutions presuppose a Supreme Being." Black,
along with Frankfurter and Jackson, voted to strike down the program, arguing that church and state must be kept "completely separate."

Douglas later recanted his "accommodationist" view of the
First Amendment and became the Court's most ardent separationist.
But at least he voted the right way in *Zorach*. Unfortunately, the
Court did not use *Zorach* to overrule *McCollum*. And soon enough
the Court resumed its project of pushing religion from the public
schools.

In *Engel v. Vitale* (1962) the Court struck down state-sponsored
school prayer.[11] In 1951 the New York State Board of Regents, in
consultation with area clergy, composed and recommended for
daily use in public schools a nondenominational prayer of twenty-
two words: "Almighty God, we acknowledge our dependence upon

10. 343 U.S. 306 (1952).
11. 370 U.S. 421 (1962).

Thee, and we beg Thy blessings upon us, our parents, our teachers and our Country." Officials justified the prayer as a part of a child's moral and spiritual training. Student participation was voluntary. New York courts said that the Regents prayer passed muster because students weren't compelled to join in. But the Supreme Court sided with the separationists who brought the case. Writing for the majority, Justice Black said it was beside the point that students weren't forced to participate, because the ban on establishing religion "does not depend on any showing of direct government compulsion." What offended the First Amendment, he continued, was that the state had engaged in religious activity by writing a prayer. And under the establishment clause, government is "without power to prescribe by law any particular form of prayer which is to be used as an official prayer in carrying on any program of governmentally sponsored religious activity." Only Justice Potter Stewart dissented.

Evidently worried about negative public reaction, Black said that the decision did not evince "hostility to religion." He wrote that the framers of the First Amendment wanted to get government out of the business of "writing or sanctioning official prayers." But Black did not address the fact that the First Congress, which proposed the Bill of Rights, also elected a chaplain who was surely expected to say prayers. Or that it passed a resolution asking the president "to recommend to the people of the United States a day of public thanksgiving and prayer, to be observed by acknowledging, with grateful hearts, the many signal favors of Almighty God." The resolution didn't include an actual prayer but stated what its substance should be—substance strikingly similar to that found more than 170 years later in the Regents prayer.

Though supportive of the decision, the *New Republic* was puzzled that the Court accepted *Engel* for review, since school prayer was not an issue being pressed in the lower courts. Yet the magazine conceded the effect of the ruling, which was to "give recognition to the relatively recent phenomenon of a widespread secular humanism in the country which constitutes, as it were, a new religion of its own."

A year later the Court reaffirmed *Engel* when it struck down Bible reading and recitation of the Lord's Prayer in cases from Pennsylvania and Maryland that were decided together as *Abington v. Schempp* (1963).[12] Neither state required student participation in the activities—a fact of no importance to the Court. Justice Tom Clark said that the establishment clause requires "neutrality" between government and religion and explained that for a law to pass constitutional muster, it must have "a secular legislative purpose and a primary effect that neither advances nor inhibits religion." That twofold requirement, by the way, soon mutated into the so-called *Lemon* test (discussed below) for determining whether a state action violates the establishment clause.

In dissent Justice Stewart took issue with Clark's understanding of neutrality, contending that "permission of such exercises for those who want them is necessary if the schools are truly to be neutral in the matter of religion." Moreover, he said, "a refusal to permit religious exercises" constitutes "the establishment of a religion of secularism." A defensive Clark responded: "We do not agree . . . that this decision in any sense has that effect." Yet Clark declined to explain why that was so. In a lengthy concurrence Justice William Brennan elaborated his view that government acts unconstitutionally if it "uses religious means to serve secular ends when secular means would suffice." For Brennan, "strict neutrality" must operate strictly—against religion.

Justice Stewart noticed that the majority's "doctrinaire reading of the establishment clause" had led to "irreconcilable conflict with the free exercise clause." He reminded his brethren of the Court's oft-stated duty "to render [challenged activities] constitutional if

12. 374 U.S. 203 (1963).

reasonably possible." He pointed out that the Court could have held the activities constitutional on the understanding that public schools in the two states would have to accommodate requests for other religious exercises. "It is conceivable," he wrote, "that these school boards, or even all school boards, might eventually find it impossible to administer a system of religious exercises during school hours in such a way as to meet this constitutional standard—in such a way as to completely free from any kind of official coercion those who do not affirmatively want to participate. But I think we must not assume that school boards so lack the qualities of inventiveness and good will as to make impossible the achievement of that goal."

In *Stone v. Graham* (1980) the Court held unconstitutional a Kentucky law requiring the posting of the Ten Commandments in the state's public schools.[13] For the Court, it didn't matter that voluntary, private contributions underwrote the posted copies of the Ten Commandments, nor that the Bible verses were not read aloud, as in the Maryland case reviewed in *Schempp*, since, of course, they were simply posted on walls. Concluding that the law had not a secular but a religious purpose, the Court worried that students might read, even "meditate upon, perhaps . . . venerate and obey" the Ten Commandments.

In *Wallace v. Jaffree* (1985), the Court struck down an Alabama law authorizing public schools to set aside a one-minute period of silence "for meditation or voluntary prayer."[14] The Court cited the intent of the law's chief sponsor in the legislature to "return voluntary prayer" to the public schools as evidence that the law lacked a secular purpose. Such an intent, declared the Court, is "quite different from [the intent] merely [to protect] every student's right to engage in voluntary prayer during an appropriate

13. 449 U.S. 39 (1980).
14. 472 U.S. 38 (1985).

moment of silence during the school day." Presumably, a moment-of-silence law drafted without "bad intent" is constitutional.

In *Lee v. Weisman* (1992), a case from Providence, Rhode Island, the Court extended its school prayer decisions to hold that the state may not direct "the performance of religious activity" at school promotional and graduation ceremonies.[15] The "religious activity" happened to be the sort of prayers traditionally offered at such ceremonies—an invocation and a benediction. And the performance of that activity was carried out by area clergy of diverse faiths. The Court found that the school district's supervision of such ceremonies created pressure, albeit "subtle and indirect," on "attending students to stand as a group or, at least, maintain respectful silence" while the prayers were said. In the creation of that pressure the Court discerned an establishment of religion. "The state may not," the justices concluded, "place primary and secondary school children in this position."

Eight years later the Court invoked *Lee* in striking down student-led prayers before high school football games.[16] Under rules established by the school district in Sante Fe, Texas, student elections were used to decide whether pregame prayers should be said and, if so, which students would offer the prayers. Writing for the Court, Justice John Paul Stevens found in those arrangements "state sponsorship of a religious message" that is impermissible because "it sends the ancillary message to members of the audience who are non-adherents that they are outsiders, not full members of the political community, and an accompanying message to adherents that they are insiders, favored members of the political community." Sante Fe was guilty of coercing football fans readying themselves for the kickoff "to participate in an act of religious worship" that they might find "personally offensive." In dissent Justice Rehn-

15. 505 U.S. 577 (1992).
16. *Sante Fe Independent School District v. Jane Doe*, 530 U.S. 290 (2000).

quist wrote that the majority opinion "bristles with hostility to all things religious in public life."

The banishing of religion from the public schools hasn't pleased most Americans, to judge by surveys of public opinion taken down through the years. *Engel* and *Schempp* in particular have drawn the most sustained objection. Many efforts have been made either to amend the Constitution or to enact statutory law that would allow room for voluntary prayers or other religious activities in the public schools. Consider, for example, the "moment of silence" statutes passed in many states (constitutional so long as they conform to *Jaffree*). But the only successful effort at the federal level came in 1984, with the passage of the Equal Access Act, which requires public high schools receiving federal funds to allow student-led religious groups to meet (and engage in religious activity such as prayer and Bible study) on the same basis and under the same conditions as any other student-led group. When a Nebraska public high school refused "equal access" to a student-led religious group, a lawsuit ensued, alleging that the school had violated the new law. In *Westside v. Mergens* (1990), the Court rejected the argument that permitting access would amount to an establishment of religion.[17] The Court was persuaded that because individual students chose to participate in a fellowship of religious believers who were also students, the school itself was not endorsing religion.

Public Aid to Church-Related Schools

Twenty-one years after the *Everson* case, the Court returned to the issue of school aid in *Board of Education v. Allen* (1968).[18] Here the Court sustained a New York statute requiring local schools to lend textbooks free of charge to students in grades seven to twelve.

17. 496 U.S. 226 (1990).
18. 392 U.S. 236 (1968).

It did not matter which schools—public or private, including religious—the students attended. The books dealt with secular subjects only, had to be approved by public school authorities, and were lent directly to the students. The Court found that the law was not unconstitutional because it passed the test devised in *Abington v. Schempp* (1963) for determining an establishment-clause violation. That test was understood by the Schempp Court in 1963 as a way of effectuating the separationist doctrine of *Everson.* Writing for the Court in *Allen,* Justice Byron White said that the parochial school bus law upheld in *Everson* and the textbook-lending law now under review met the two parts of the test, for both statutes had "a secular legislative purpose and a primary effect that neither advances nor inhibits religion." Justice Black disagreed, finding the law "a flat, flagrant, open violation" of the Constitution.

Three years after *Allen* the Court decided *Lemon v. Kurtzman* (1971).[19] At issue were state laws that paid the salaries of teachers of secular subjects in church-related schools. The Court did not find that the laws lacked a secular purpose or that their primary effect was to advance or inhibit religion. But the Court added a third element to its analysis—whether a given law fosters an "excessive government entanglement" with religion. Thus was born the *Lemon* test, and the laws challenged in *Lemon* were the first to fail it. The Court said the states would have to monitor what the teachers they paid were doing, since they might teach not only math, say, but also faith and morals, and yet such monitoring would entangle public authorities excessively with religious matters.

For more than a decade, the Court continued to apply the *Lemon* test, or variants thereof, in school aid cases. The Court ruled against public aid provided directly to church-related elementary and secondary schools, even when the purpose of the aid was secular and its use carefully monitored. Citing the religious dimension

19. 403 U.S. 602 (1970).

of the schools' mission, the Court saw the schools as "pervasively sectarian" and concluded that the primary effect of public aid given to them directly would be to advance religion. When states designed grants so that the money could be spent only for specific educational purposes unrelated to the schools' religious goals, the Court said that the monitoring needed to keep track of how the money was being spent excessively entangled the state with religion.

In 1985 the Court again applied the *Lemon* test in *Aguilar v. Felton*.[20] Under review was Title I of the Elementary and Secondary Education Act of 1965, which provided funds to public schools for remedial education. Children with learning disabilities were eligible for the assistance regardless of whether they attended public or private (including religious) schools. To implement Title I, public school teachers had for years entered the parochial schools to teach eligible children. That fact doomed the program for a majority of the justices. As they saw it, having public school teachers actually inside parochial schools constituted an excessive state entanglement with religion.

Legal scholar Kermit Hall has called *Aguilar* "something of a high-water mark" in the Court's effort "to drive a clear constitutional wedge" between church and state.[21] Yet in time *Aguilar* would be overruled. Unable to send their teachers into church-related schools, public school authorities responded to *Aguilar* by resorting to expensive and awkward alternatives. New York City, where *Aguilar* was litigated, wound up spending most of its federal education aid to lease vans that, parked near the parochial schools, served as mobile classrooms for more than twenty thousand students attending those schools. The Reagan, Bush, and Clinton administrations objected to the practical difficulties that *Aguilar*

20. 473 U.S. 402 (1985).
21. Kermit Hall, ed., *The Oxford Guide to United States Supreme Court Decisions* (New York: Oxford University Press, 1999), 7.

had created for the implementation of Title I—as did many school districts across the nation. Eventually the New York City school board decided to challenge the court order in *Aguilar* under which it still labored. The case was litigated at a propitious moment, for since *Aguilar* the Court had repudiated the notion that all aid underwriting secular education in church-related schools is unconstitutional. In *Agostini v. Felton* (1997), the Court abandoned its previous view that "the placement of public employees on parochial school grounds inevitably results" in a violation of the First Amendment.[22] *Agostini* thus permitted the very arrangement that *Aguilar* had condemned.

In *Mitchell v. Helms* (2000), the Court refused to follow separationist precedents as it sustained a federal law authorizing the subsidization of library, media, and computer materials for public and private (including religious) schools.[23] Decisions from the mid-1970s counseled the opposite result, and in previous cases as many as six different justices had expressed a willingness to overrule them. Yet in *Mitchell*, Justice Clarence Thomas, who wrote for three other justices, was unable to gain a fifth vote for repudiating the proposition that, to satisfy the establishment clause, "pervasively sectarian schools" must by reason of their character be excluded from otherwise valid aid programs.

The Court also has approved public assistance provided *directly* to students attending church-related schools. In *Mueller v. Allen* (1983), the Court sustained a Minnesota law allowing taxpayers to deduct from their state taxable income up to $700 per child for tuition, textbook, and school transportation expenses, regardless of whether they attended public or private schools.[24] Almost all of those taking the deduction were parents of children enrolled in church-related schools. In *Zelman v. Simmons-Harris* (2002), the

22. 117 S. Ct. 1332 (1997).
23. 530 U.S. 793 (2000).
24. 463 U.S. 388 (1983).

Court upheld an Ohio program authorizing publicly financed vouchers for use in sending students to church-related elementary and secondary schools.[25] The vouchers were designed to help children in low-income families living in Cleveland and could be used at public or private—including church-related—schools. The vouchers were provided directly to eligible parents, who were able, as Chief Justice Rehnquist wrote in his opinion for the Court, "to exercise genuine choice among options public and private, secular and religious." Rehnquist concluded that the program was "neutral" and did not unconstitutionally advance religion. It was left to Justice Stevens, author of the Court's opinions in *Jaffree* and *Sante Fe*, to complain in dissent that "whenever we remove a brick from the wall that was designed to separate religion and government, we increase the risk of religious strife and weaken the foundation of democracy."

Over the years the Court has regarded church-related colleges and universities as not only inculcating religious beliefs but also teaching critical thinking skills, and it has viewed college-age students as less "impressionable" than younger students. For these reasons, the Court has been willing to uphold state aid directly given to religious colleges. Nor has the Court found a violation of the establishment clause when a college-age student uses state-provided vocational education funds to attend a Bible college and prepare for the ministry. In *Witters v. Washington* (1986), the Court unanimously embraced the principle of neutrality: How college-age students might use public educational funds for which they are eligible should be of no concern to the state. Choice of school and career goals—religious or secular—must be left entirely to the students.

25. 536 U.S. 639 (2002).

Other "Establishments" of Religion

From the nation's founding our public life has included various acknowledgments and accommodations of religious belief. Once the Court began deciding religion cases in the way it did, its separationist doctrine fraught with far-reaching implications, it was inevitable that plaintiffs would emerge seeking to effect what Richard Neuhaus has called "a public square naked of religious symbol and substance."[26]

One of the first cases concerned state and local laws requiring the closing on Sunday of all but the most essential businesses. The so-called "blue laws" dated from the colonial period and had undeniable religious origins, inasmuch as they were intended both to recognize the Sabbath and to encourage church attendance. But in *McGowan v. Maryland* (1961) the Court, declining to condemn such laws on account of their religious origins, sustained them because of the secular purpose they now served—that they provided a day of rest that anyone could take advantage of, in whatever way the person wanted.[27]

Nine years later in *Walz v. Tax Commission* (1970) the Court upheld tax exemptions for churches, a policy dating from the colonial period and adhered to by all fifty states and the federal government.[28] If it now seems hard to imagine that the Court might have struck down a policy of such vintage and universal acceptance, bear in mind that in *Everson* the Court did say that "neither a state nor the federal government can . . . pass laws which . . . aid all religions." Tax exemptions for churches plainly aided "all religions," a point the majority opinion didn't deny. Tax exemptions were unconstitutional, if that part of *Everson* controlled. But

26. See Richard John Neuhaus, *The Naked Public Square* (Grand Rapids: Wm. B. Erdmans, 1984).

27. 336 U.S. 470 (1961).

28. 397 U.S. 664 (1970).

not even Justice Black was willing to apply the case in that way. Only Justice Douglas, who in *Zorach* had declared that "we are a religious people whose institutions presuppose a Supreme Being," said that tax exemptions constituted an unconstitutional "subsidy" of religion.

In *Marsh v. Chambers* (1983), the Court sustained another practice of two centuries' standing—the legislative chaplaincy.[29] The U.S. Court of Appeals for the Eighth Circuit had duly applied the *Lemon* test in striking down Nebraska's chaplaincy. Justice Brennan, had he commanded a majority, would have found the chaplaincy in violation of all three parts of the test. Presumably, Chief Justice Burger would also have been compelled to vote against the chaplaincy had he applied the test—of which he had been the author. Writing for the majority, Burger declined to use the test and instead argued from the "unambiguous and unbroken history of more than 200 years" of federal and state chaplaincies to uphold the Nebraska arrangement.

In *Lynch v. Donnelly* (1984) and *County of Allegheny v. ACLU* (1989), the Court addressed the constitutionality of holiday displays.[30] In *Lynch*, the city of Pawtucket, Rhode Island, erected a Christmas display that included a Santa Claus house, reindeer pulling Santa's sleigh, a Christmas tree, and a clown, as well as a crèche consisting of the baby Jesus, Mary and Joseph, angels, shepherds and kings, and animals. The Court applied the *Lemon* test (not used the year before in *Marsh*) in concluding that in the context of the display, the crèche was constitutional since it had a secular purpose, didn't advance or inhibit religion, and didn't excessively entangle the state in religion. Five years later in *Allegheny*, the Court said that a crèche not surrounded by other, more secular, objects could not be placed in a public building without

29. 463 U.S. 783 (1983).
30. 465 U.S. 668 (1984); 492 U.S. 573 (1989).

violating the establishment clause. A menorah, however, won the approval of the Court—because secular symbols were placed close to it.

In *Elk Grove Unified School District v. Newdow* (2004), Michael Newdow, an atheist opposed to any trace of religion in the public square, took aim at the words "under God" in the Pledge of Allegiance. Congress had added the two words to the Pledge in 1954, and his daughter attended a California public school where students were given the opportunity (but not required) to recite the pledge each day. Newdow sued Congress and the school district, alleging that both governments were in violation of the establishment clause. The Ninth Circuit agreed with both claims. Reviewing only the challenge to the school district, the Supreme Court concluded that Newdow lacked standing to bring his lawsuit.[31] The Court thus did not reach the merits of the constitutional issue. Still, what's notable about the *Newdow* case is its inevitability, for under the Court's various establishment-clause tests (*Lemon*, "endorsement of religion," "coercion") the 1954 Pledge would seem clearly in violation of the First Amendment. Someone committed to a completely secular public square was going to pursue a case based on the Court's precedents, and Newdow did. Someone else will follow him, and someday the Court might decide the "under God" question. Because of the precedents, the only way the Pledge might be saved is for a majority to disregard the law and to construe "under God" (disingenuously) as lacking any serious religious meaning. Thus did Justice Sandra Day O'Connor write separately in *Newdow* to say that she would have upheld "under God" as "ceremonial deism." Likewise, in his separate opinion, Justice Rehnquist said he would have upheld the words as "a patriotic observance."

31. No. 02-1624 (2004).

"No Law . . . Prohibiting the
Free Exercise Thereof"

One of the few religion cases decided before *Cantwell v. Connecticut* (1940) was *Reynolds v. United States* (1879).[32] Acting under a federal antibigamy statute, the government sought to end Mormon polygamy in what was then the territory of Utah. George Reynolds, secretary to Brigham Young, was convicted of bigamy. The Supreme Court declined to reverse, rejecting Reynolds's argument that he should be exempted from the law because his faith taught that he could take more than one wife. The Court distinguished between belief and action: government may not punish citizens for their religious beliefs but may regulate religiously motivated actions—in this case Reynolds's bigamy—if it has a rational basis for doing so. Rare is the government unable to demonstrate a "rational" basis for what it does.

Reynolds remained the law until *Sherbert v. Verner* (1963).[33] Adell Sherbert, a Seventh-Day Adventist, was fired by her South Carolina employer because she refused to work on Saturday, the Sabbath of her faith. Unable to find a job where she wouldn't have to work on Saturday, she filed for unemployment compensation. South Carolina rejected her claim on the ground that she was ineligible for such benefits because she had refused to accept suitable work that included Saturday employment. Sherbert went to court, alleging a violation of the free exercise clause. Not surprisingly, given the law of *Reynolds*, the South Carolina Supreme Court held for the state. But the U.S. Supreme Court reversed, holding that South Carolina had forced Sherbert to "choose between following the precepts of her religion and forfeiting benefits, on the one hand, and abandoning one of the precepts of her religion in order to

32. 98 U.S. 145 (1979).
33. 374 U.S. 398 (1963).

accept work, on the other." The Court asked whether the state had some "compelling interest" that might sustain its action and concluded that it had none. *Sherbert* produced new doctrine: Government actions that substantially burden a religious practice must be justified by a compelling governmental interest. If government has no such interest, then it must create an exemption for the conduct.

Sherbert was followed by *Wisconsin v. Yoder* (1972).[34] At issue was a Wisconsin law requiring parents of all children to send them to private or public schools until they reached age sixteen. Some Amish parents refused to send their children, ages fourteen and fifteen, beyond the eighth grade. They justified their action through their faith. Convicted of violating the compulsory-attendance law, the parents sued on free exercise grounds. The Court, unable to credit Wisconsin with a compelling interest, agreed with them. The irony of the case was that the exemption the Court demanded for the Amish might well have been declared an unconstitutional establishment of religion had the Wisconsin legislature enacted it.

The Court limited the reach of *Sherbert* in *Employment Division v. Smith* (1990).[35] Alfred Smith and Galen Black ingested the hallucinogenic drug peyote during an American Indian church ceremony in which the drug was sacramentally used. Smith and Black, who worked with a private drug-rehabilitation organization, were then fired from their jobs for using the drug. When they filed for unemployment compensation, Oregon judged them ineligible for benefits because they had been fired for work-related "misconduct"—ingestion of peyote, possession of which is a felony in that state. Smith and Black challenged the state's decision on free exercise grounds, seeking an exemption from otherwise valid law. But a five-justice majority held for Oregon. "[A]n individual's religious

34. 406 U.S. 205 (1972).
35. 494 U.S. 872 (1990).

beliefs," wrote Justice Antonin Scalia for the Court, "[do not] excuse him from compliance with an otherwise valid law prohibiting conduct that the State is free to regulate."

Scalia declined to apply *Sherbert*'s demand that Oregon produce a compelling interest in support of its denial to Smith and Black of unemployment compensation. Scalia expressed concern that requiring a compelling interest in a case like *Smith* would produce "a private right to ignore generally applicable law." Scalia's position—that "generally applicable, religion-neutral laws that have the effect of burdening a particular religious practice need not be justified by a compelling governmental interest"—meant that legislatures, not courts, would mainly decide whether conduct exemptions might be warranted. Central to Scalia's objection to the compelling interest standard was that courts would "constantly be in the business" of deciding which conduct exemptions might be warranted. In 1991—as the legislatures of Arizona, Colorado, and New Mexico had done earlier—the Oregon legislature voted to make an exception to its drug law for sacramental peyote use.

Smith led to federal legislation creating a more stringent test in evaluating free exercise claims. The Religious Freedom Restoration Act of 1993 was passed by unanimous vote in the House and with only three votes against in the Senate. A Catholic church in Boerne, Texas, reached for the help of the new law when city officials denied it permission to enlarge its building in a neighborhood zoned for historic preservation. In *City of Boerne v. Flores* (1997) the Supreme Court found that Congress had exceeded its constitutional authority in passing the statute.[36] *Smith* remained good law, and the task of carving out exemptions for religiously based conduct remained with legislatures.

Smith, of course, did not say what the free exercise clause actually demands of government. In 1993 the Court began to fill in that

36. 521 U.S. 507 (1997).

blank. At issue in *Church of the Lukumi Babalu Aye, Inc. v. Hialeah* was a Florida city's effort to render illegal the practice of the Santería religion.[37] The Court unanimously struck down regulations that did not mention the religion as such but were clearly aimed at outlawing its rituals, which involve animal sacrifice. The free exercise clause, said the Court, means that government may not suppress specific religious practices.

Also in 1993 the Court reviewed another free exercise question in *Lamb's Chapel v. Center Moriches Union Free School District*.[38] Lamb's Chapel applied for after-hour use of school facilities to show the James Dobson videos on raising Christian families. The school district denied the application, whereupon Lamb's Chapel challenged the regulations, which allowed social, civic, and recreational uses but forbade those for religious purposes. The Court unanimously held for Lamb's Chapel, but the majority relied on the First Amendment's free speech clause, not the free exercise clause: the school district had engaged in unconstitutional viewpoint discrimination by treating Lamb's Chapel differently because of its religious point of view. Given the success of Lamb's Chapel, other religious groups successfully brought cases in the 1990s claiming viewpoint discrimination.[39] Although the Court reached the right results in these cases, they have had, as Vincent Phillip Munoz points out, "a devastating effect on free exercise. Aside from the rare case in which a specific religious practice is suppressed directly"—as occurred in the *Hialeah* case—"religious free exercise has lost its independent value."[40]

In 2004 the Court had before it a new free exercise claim in

37. 508 U.S. 520 (1993).
38. 508 U.S. 384 (1993).
39. See *Rosenberger v. University of Virginia*, 515 U.S. 819 (1995) and *Good News Club v. Milford Central School*, 533 U.S. 98 (2001).
40. Munoz, "Establishing Free Exercise," 18.

Locke v. Davey (2004).[41] Joshua Davey, a high school senior in the state of Washington, won a state-funded college scholarship that could be used at any public or private college. Enrolling at Northwest College, which is affiliated with the Assemblies of God, Davey decided on a double major in business and pastoral ministries. He then received a letter from state authorities advising that by choosing the pastoral major—an exercise of faith, not a speech act, by the way—he would have to give up his scholarship. The statute authorizing the scholarship program denied the award of the aid to "any student who is pursuing a degree in theology." The statute thus sought to ensure agreement with the state constitution, which forbids public funding of "any religious worship, exercise or instruction" and declares that "all schools maintained or supported wholly or in part by the public funds shall be forever free of sectarian control." Davey sued, contending that the state violated the free exercise clause by denying theology students a benefit available to all others. By a vote of seven to two, and with Chief Justice Rehnquist writing, the Court rejected Davey's free exercise argument. Yet as Justice Scalia wrote in dissent, there can be no doubt that "this case is about discrimination against a religious minority. Most citizens of this country identify themselves as professing some religious belief, but the state's policy poses no obstacles to practitioners of only a tepid, civic version of faith. Those the statutory exclusion actually affects—those whose belief in their religion is so strong that they dedicate their study and their lives to its ministry—are a far narrower set."

No Longer the "First" Political Institution

In the *Newdow* and *Davey* cases, the Court had an opportunity to correct the egregious errors of its predecessors and finally make

41. No. 02-1315.

sense of "establishment" and "free exercise." But of course the Court did not do that. The various tests for determining an establishment of religion—the *Lemon* test, endorsement, and coercion—still remain in the Court's toolbox. So they still can be used to discriminate against religion. And the Court has yet to read the ban on establishing religion in conjunction with the prohibition of its free exercise. Perhaps it feels it does not have to, since in the Court's decisions free exercise has so little substance. But the major surgery needed to correct the Court's religion jurisprudence seems unlikely unless the Court finally decides to take free exercise seriously. Toward that end, the Court will have to inquire into its original meaning. And here a good case can be made that James Madison best captured that meaning when he wrote that no one should be extended privileges because of religion, nor subjected to penalties or disabilities. One despairs, however, of calling yet again for the Court to get the First Amendment right. The Court prefers to nibble at the edges of its jurisprudence, to revise only here and there. And meanwhile the more secular America that the Court's decisions have helped bring about remains as close to any citizen as the nearest public school.

Doubtless there are many Americans who applaud the new America, but the founders would have regarded it with grave concern. They were persuaded that the liberal state they had fashioned would be unable to produce in the people the virtues that it needed to survive, and they knew from history that most people most of the time draw their ethics, their sense of morality and justice, from their religion. Thus, in his Farewell Address George Washington reminded the young nation that religion and morality are "indispensable" to "political prosperity" and cautioned against indulging "the supposition that morality can be maintained without religion." Washington implored "the mere politician, equally with the pious man, . . . to respect and cherish" religion. Several decades later Alexis de Tocqueville captured the founders' sentiments when he

described religion as "the first of [the Americans'] political institutions" because it was "indispensable to the maintenance of [our]
republican institutions." It is not apparent that as many as five
justices now sitting on the Court would agree with this view of the
role of religion in American life. We are still embarked in a new
direction, destination unknown.

4

The New Diplomacy
Threatens American
Sovereignty and Values

David Davenport

It is difficult to turn on the television today without seeing an odd assortment of folks sitting around a casino table playing poker. Formerly a game people played rather than watched, poker has become a major television hit, with sports networks airing poker marathons to compete with popular events on other stations.

Perhaps this explains why I have come to think of international diplomacy during and after the Cold War as two very different poker tables. At the Cold War table, in operation from 1945 to 1989, sat two high-stakes players: the United States and the Soviet Union. Since this game required immense military and economic power to play, these two dominated the action. The United Nations had a lesser seat at the table, and from time to time other nations would bid up a particular hand, but the United States and the Soviet Union always held the decisive cards.

A novel aspect of televised poker is the ability of the camera to show hidden cards as players bluff and disguise their hands. It turns out that the Soviet Union, far weaker economically and militarily than the world knew, was consistently bluffing and overplaying its hand. When the United States, especially during the Reagan administration in the 1980s, increased its military strength and economic power, the weakness of the Soviet hand became evident and the Soviet Union essentially folded.

The post–Cold War table is quite different. With no nation capable of sitting across from the United States in a military and economic power contest, the nature of both the game itself and the kind and number of players began to change. For starters, many new players sought a seat at the table. Other nations wanted in the game, of course, but so did nongovernmental organizations (NGOs) of many types. International organizations, including the United Nations and newer ones such as the World Trade Organization (WTO), took what they viewed as their rightful place at the table, as did new groupings of nations such as the European Union and the "like-minded states."

Short on military and economic capital, these new players have sought to change the table to a "soft power" game. Small- and medium-sized "like-minded states" and NGOs have combined to carry out a "new diplomacy," with notable victories in enacting international treaties to ban land mines and to establish the International Criminal Court (ICC). At the same time, other expansions of international law, including the developing doctrine of universal jurisdiction, seek to move global issues away from traditional diplomatic or political arenas and into courtrooms.

In one sense, who could object to the world's changing from hard power to soft? And who would oppose the wider application of legal standards around the world? The answer to both questions is: the United States. Despite the high-sounding rhetoric about international law and soft power, the new diplomacy seeks to alter the world's political power structure and to do so in a way that presents real threats to American sovereignty and values. In the next few hands, the nature of the post–Cold War diplomatic table is likely to be decided.

International Law and Its Discontents

The United States is a nation of laws with the most highly developed legal system in the world. Some believe the United States should therefore be a natural ally in the major expansion of international law that is now under way. Such a view ignores two fundamental realities: (1) international law is entirely different from U.S. law and, by its very nature, the one impinges on the other; and (2) international law is presently being used as a tool by advocates of the new diplomacy to pursue an agenda that is antithetical to important American interests.

One way to understand the nature of international law is to contrast its philosophy with U.S. law. The American legal system essentially begins with the individual rights of each citizen expressed in the Declaration of Independence and the Bill of Rights. A major purpose of U.S. law is to protect those rights against intrusion by the government or other citizens. When necessary, some of those individual rights may be ceded to government. Even then Americans cede rights sparingly and to a level of government closest to the people: first, local, second, state, and finally, federal. Although the federal government has steadily expanded its reach in recent decades, the historical roots of the U.S. legal and political system run from the ground up, emanating from individual rights up the branches of government as necessary.

By contrast, international law, especially as it is being developed today, is essentially top-down in nature. A relatively small group of world leaders, augmented by hundreds of NGOs, decides that the world needs to ban land mines, create an aggressive international criminal court, or impose new standards about global warming. They attempt to leverage support from the United States and other nations through what new diplomacy advocates call "the mobilization of shame." The treaties go into force without the support of most nations of the world, and certainly without the agreement of nations representing most of the population of the world. In some cases, the treaties purport to apply new international law even to citizens of nations that do not sign them. This formulation and, where possible, implementation of new international law by elites, is very different from the consent-driven rule of law developed in the United States.

Of course America's traditional European allies are much more comfortable with this top-down development of law. Even America's closest friend, Great Britain, had a royal tradition to its lawmaking that is quite foreign to the American system. When critics of the U.S. approach wonder how we can be so out of step with Britain and other democratic allies about these new diplomacy treaties, it is clear that they have forgotten their American history. "Taxation without representation" was the bitter fruit of an unrepresentative English system, and the Revolutionary War was largely fought over such differences. Further, the current development of the European Union, in which individual nations cede important powers to the group, underscores that Europe is still committed to a very different approach from the American tradition of individual rights and bottom-up democracy.

Another way in which international law differs from the U.S. rule of law is that international law has no constitution or overarching set of principles; instead it attempts to codify and enforce international politics as they are, or as the proponents of a change wish them to be. As the French writer Maurice Bourquin noted, "International law is the crystallization of international politics." Indeed, some have argued that it is a misnomer to refer to international "law" since the term implies something far more concrete and enforceable than what travels under that banner.[1] With no con-

---

1. John R. Bolton, "Is There Really 'Law' in International Affairs?" *Transnational Law and Contemporary Problems* 10 (Spring 2000): 1. See also Robert H. Bork, "The Limits of International Law," *The National Interest* (Winter 1989–1990): 3.

stitution to set forth international legal principles, no community to particularize them into laws, and no executive to enforce them, international law is not at all like the U.S. concept of the rule of law.

What international law is, and what we are seeing in this recent expansion, is essentially one tool in the kit of diplomatic power. In a sense, international law is only what the powerful nations of the time agree it is and are willing to enforce. For example, the U.S. and allied bombing of targets in Kosovo in 1999 did not have U.N. Security Council approval and therefore, under the U.N. Charter, presumably violated international law. Nevertheless, the major world powers agreed that was a good thing to do and any violation of international law never became a major issue. International law is also a tool to which weaker nations may resort, in the absence of other forms of power, while more powerful nations may prefer other tools.[2]

More specifically, the present expansion of international law is about small- and medium-sized states—mostly Canada and the European Union nations—joining with human rights NGOs to pursue a particular political agenda. It is to these players, the new diplomacy processes they are using, their agenda, and the effect on U.S. sovereignty and values that we now turn.

New Players Change the Table

The biggest change in post–Cold War diplomacy is the addition of nonstate actors, especially NGOs, to the bargaining table.[3] Various figures about their growth have been cited and they are all impressive. Before World War I, for example, there were 176 international NGOs. By 1956, there were nearly 1,000, and by 1970 nearly

2. Paul W. Kahn, "Speaking Law to Power," *Chicago Journal of International Law* 1 (1) (2000): 1.

3. See Jessica T. Mathews, "Power Shift," *Foreign Affairs* 76 (1) (1997): 50.

2,000. One source estimates that during the 1990s international NGOs grew from 5,000 to 27,000, while another suggests that these organizations quadrupled in the last decade so that there are now more than 50,000 of them.[4]

It is not just the quantity of these NGOs that is significant but also the role they now play in international diplomacy. In their early days NGOs were limited to providing advocacy and support in diplomatic hallways. In the past decade, however, they have moved from the hallway to the diplomatic table and have not only advocated but provided the main leadership and drafting of several treaties. About 1000 NGOs were front and center in the Ottawa Process leading to the treaty to ban land mines, and NGO leader Jody Williams won a share of the Nobel Prize for those efforts. Similarly NGO leader William Pace is acknowledged as the principal coordinator in the development of the ICC.

Nongovernmental organizations have not just joined the diplomatic table, but in treaties such as those banning land mines and establishing the ICC, they have supplanted the leadership of traditional world powers and, to some degree, even nation-states. As Professors Diana Tussie and Maria Pia Riggirozzi have noted: "NGOs have kicked at the doors and wriggled into the closed rooms of international negotiations. Chipping in at the sides of state power, in many instances they have altered daily operational procedures and priorities."[5] For example, the U.S. delegation was left out of the final negotiations on the ICC at the Rome conference in 1998 and, like other countries, was presented a "take it or leave it" package by NGOs and their colleagues from the like-minded

---

4. See Joseph S. Nye Jr., *The Paradox of American Power* (Oxford: Oxford University Press, 2002): 60. See also Edith Brown Weiss, "The Rise or the Fall of International Law?" *Fordham Law Review* 69 (November 2000): 350; and Daniel W. Drezner, "On the Balance Between International Law and Democratic Sovereignty," *Chicago Journal of International Law* 2 (2) (2001): 322.

5. Volker Rittberger, ed., *Global Governance and the United Nations System* (Tokyo: United Nations Press, 2001): 175.

states.[6] The ICC has moved ahead without ratification by the United States, Russia, Japan, India, China, and other major powers. The NGO leadership at the diplomatic table—a role previously reserved for nation-states—is problematic in several respects. For one thing, NGOs tend to be narrowly focused on a single issue, less concerned with the balancing of interests required of policy leaders. Unlike states, NGOs are not charged with juggling jobs, a national debt, and a variety of spending priorities. NGOs are largely formed to pursue a single mission, such as banning land mines, or a package of purposes, such as human rights. Their style is generally more one of debate and confrontation than compromise. This makes them excellent advocates but not balanced leaders of an international legal process. NGOs would sacrifice a wide range of procedural measures or legal niceties in order to enact treaties that further their agenda. Americans who would be suspicious of such single-issue groups in the United States should be doubly concerned about their influence in the undemocratic international arena.

A related problem is that nearly all NGOs participating in the development of these new international treaties are on one side of the issue. At meetings about the ICC, basically, all the NGOs in attendance favor an aggressive international criminal court, just as NGOs in Ottawa overwhelmingly supported the enactment of a rapid and total ban of land mines. There is also considerable anti-American sentiment among these NGOs, which is somewhat ironic since the largest number of NGOs is based in the United States and receives heavy funding from U.S. donors. Consequently, granting these new actors power at the diplomatic table has had a lopsided political effect in favor of aggressive new treaties and against U.S. foreign policy.

6. David Scheffer, "Developments in International Law: The United States and the International Criminal Court," *American Journal of International Law* 93 (1) (1999): 20.

Finally, NGOs do not have the sort of accountability that would
be expected of leaders developing international law.[7] NGOs work
from their own local base directly into the international arena, skip-
ping over the national level with its give and take or checks and
balances system of democratic accountability. Indeed, it is ironic
that U.S.-based NGOs are attempting, with some success, to put
policies into effect internationally that they could not enact in their
own country. They are accountable, finally, only to those donors
who provide their funding. One participant in the Rome conference
on the ICC asked a relevant question: "Who elected these NGOs
anyway?" The answer, of course, is that, unlike the leaders of
nation-states, they elected themselves.

Joining NGOs in leading the recent expansion of international
law have been the "like-minded states." These are essentially
medium-sized and smaller states such as Canada, Australia, and the
members of the European Union that have been eager to play a
larger role on the diplomatic scene. When he served as Canada's
foreign minister, Lloyd Axworthy gave great impetus to the new
diplomacy by hosting the Ottawa Conference, which stepped out
of the normal international arms control processes and sought a
fast-track treaty to ban land mines. When that collaboration of
NGOs and like-minded states succeeded, these groups continued
their efforts in Rome to create an aggressive new model for an
international criminal court. The like-minded states have teamed
with the NGOs to create a powerful new presence at the diplomatic
table.

7. P. J. Simmons, "Learning to Live with NGOs," *Foreign Policy* 112 (Fall
1998): 82. See also "NGO, Heal Thyself!" *Foreign Policy* 135 (March/April 2003):
16.

The New, New
Diplomacy Game

There's a new game in town.[8] With the closing down of the Cold War table, and its predictable two-player military and economic power game, NGOs and small and medium-sized states have attempted to reshape the diplomatic table and introduce a new game. Though styled in idealistic terms—soft power, the rule of international law—the new diplomacy game is merely global politics by other means. The practitioners of the new diplomacy have been quite successful in the early rounds.

The new diplomacy is essentially pursuing an aggressive human rights agenda through attempted expansion of international law. The game, as it has been played out in the adoption of the land mines treaty and the development of the ICC, has several distinctive characteristics.

First the new diplomacy takes an objective being pursued by normal diplomatic processes and moves things in a different direction and on a faster track. Arms control negotiations, under the aegis of the U.N., were already under way on the problem of land-mines. The U.N. Convention on Certain Conventional Weapons (CCW) and the U.N. Conference on Disarmament in Geneva had been formulated for just such a purpose. However, these conventional approaches were moving too slowly, and their objective—limitations on land mines rather than an outright ban—was too narrow for human rights advocates. Instead Canadian Foreign Minister Lloyd Axworthy and two major NGOs—the International Campaign to Ban Landmines and the International Committee of the Red Cross—called their own convention in Ottawa where they

8. See David Davenport, "The New Diplomacy," *Policy Review* 116 (December 2002/January 2003). See also Andrew F. Cooper et al., eds., *Enhancing Global Governance: Towards a New Diplomacy* (Tokyo: United Nations University Press, 2002).

could control a different agenda: a treaty implementing a ban of land mines to be adopted in the record time of fifteen months.[9]

Similarly, an international criminal court had been in the works for decades, having been accelerated following the ad hoc tribunals for Rwanda and the former Yugoslavia.[10] The United Nations had logically commissioned the International Law Commission (ILC) to draft a proposal for such a court, and the United States and other world powers were deeply involved and supportive. Once again, however, human rights activists were not satisfied with the direction of the ILC's proposals and wanted a much broader authority for the court on a faster timetable.[11] In Rome, a newly formed NGO, the Coalition for the International Criminal Court, and the like-minded states shoved the ILC proposal aside and advocated a court of much broader jurisdiction.[12] No one expected a treaty to be approved in the short time of the Rome conference, but again the new diplomacy worked on a fast track and succeeded in producing a treaty.

A second tactic of the new diplomacy game is to supplant the normal consensus-based processes of international law with a no-reservations, take-it-or-leave-it treaty that seeks support from a coalition of the willing. In the case of the ICC, for example, the U.N. had commissioned the International Law Commission to develop a proposal that would achieve the widest possible consensus.[13] Instead NGOs and the like-minded nations preferred a stronger

    9. See Maxwell A. Cameron et al., eds., *To Walk Without Fear* (Oxford: Oxford University Press, 1998).
    10. See Herman von Hebel, "An International Criminal Court: A Historical Perspective," in *Reflections on the International Criminal Court* (The Hague: Klewer Law International, 1999): 13.
    11. See Leila Nadya Sadat, *The International Criminal Court and the Transformation of International Law* (Transnational Publishers, 2002): 40–42, 79.
    12. John Rosenthal, "A Lawless Global Court," *Policy Review* 123 (February/March 2004): 32–35.
    13. Ibid.

court with less support. Rather than seek consensus, both the land mines and ICC conventions simply took a vote. Both treaties precluded the possibility of a nation's signing with reservations, a standard part of international law confirmed in the Vienna Convention on the Law of Treaties.[14] Both treaties went into force without the support of the majority of the nations of the world, representing well under half the world's population.

Other aspects of the new diplomacy game attempt to play away from the traditional power-based approach to international relations. Lobbying and marketing have been introduced to treaty negotiations through the new diplomacy process. The various efforts of the new diplomacy are characterized by the terms "participation," "empowerment," "people-centered," and "consensus." Indeed, new diplomacy drafts are circulated as "consensus documents." In Ottawa, NGOs flooded delegates with faxes, e-mail messages, and calls to their cell phones. Daily displays showed the horror of land mines. Canadian Foreign Minister Axworthy openly referred to the campaign as "the mobilization of shame," a refrain that has been repeated in other human rights efforts.

The United States has been slow to respond to the new diplomacy approach. By the time the United States articulated the changes it would need to support the land mines treaty, advocates were already locked into their positions. The U.S. delegation accomplished some changes to the Rome Treaty for the ICC but still ended up on the losing end of a lopsided vote for the treaty. President Clinton was ambivalent about the treaties, but President Bush has been strongly opposed. Ironically, the United States is characterized as isolationist and out of step for not supporting these new diplomacy victories when, in fact, proponents of the treaties knew they were advocating aggressive agreements that the United States would not approve. In the end, the new diplomacy advocates

14. Vienna Convention on the Law of Treaties, May 22, 1969, art. 19.

wanted the treaty their way, with or without international support, including that of the United States.

A Three-Way Expansion of International Law

Those keeping score on the new diplomacy game should watch for expansions of international law in three areas: (1) treaty-based law; (2) universal jurisdiction, as part of customary international law; and (3) international organizations and global governance. New diplomacy players are working for breakthroughs in all these aspects of international law. Taken together, these reforms could well revolutionize international law at the expense of state sovereignty.

If international law is largely soft and symbolic in comparison with U.S. law, treaty-based law is the firmest of the lot. Although states may give up some part of their sovereignty when they sign and ratify a treaty, they have nevertheless made their own sovereign decision to do so. Advocates of the new diplomacy expansion of international law have found a number of ways, some old and some new, to advance their agenda through treaties.

The treaty agenda over the last decade has become a very active one. New diplomacy advocates have figured out that, rather than raise an issue before the U.N. General Assembly, it makes more sense to call a conference on the matter, where they control the guest list and the program. The model for this approach was the 1992 Conference on Environment and Development in Rio de Janeiro, which brought a crowd of NGOs and produced an aggressive environmental regulatory agenda. Of course this has been followed by a host of conferences such as the one in Kyoto on global warming, the Ottawa Convention on land mines, and so on. These conferences produce a lot of heat and passion and often a draft of a treaty as well, focused generally on human rights, the environment, sustainable development, or other new diplomacy agenda items.

Even though treaties are generally only applicable to signatory states, they nevertheless have an impact on the diplomatic and policy environment. For one thing, they set the agenda that the world will discuss. In the case of land mines, for example, the normal arms control processes were focused on limitations, but the Ottawa Convention changed the conversation to a total ban. Kyoto set standards for global warming which then became the topics to which others must react. By being the first and most passionate statements in their field, these treaties develop a set of global expectations. Treaties also provide a standard for the new diplomacy's "blame, shame and name" approach in which countries that do not sign or follow the treaty become objects of attack. Russia experienced this recently when it signaled that it may not ratify the Kyoto accord on global warming. Its reasoning was much like that of the United States, which has not signed on. It is not that they oppose treaties—an accusation routinely made against the United States—but that the Kyoto accord poses dangers to Russian economic growth and may do little for the environment. Finally, Russia succumbed to the shame campaign and ratified the treaty. The globalists rarely accept that a nation may have strategic reasons or other priorities for refusing to ratify or follow a treaty.

These recent treaties pack another surprising punch. Both the land mines treaty and the Rome Treaty for the International Criminal Court do not allow nations to state reservations when they sign and ratify. The ability of a nation to express reservations and exceptions to parts of a treaty has been a standard part of international law, confirmed in the Vienna Convention on the Law of Treaties. This feature has allowed nations, such as the United States, to sign treaties they otherwise would not sign, by accepting the treaty in part but stating reservations to other sections. This novel assertion, which flies in the face of international law, is a bold one and it remains to be seen whether it will be accepted.

Bolder and more expansive still, the treaty creating the ICC purports to give the court jurisdiction over citizens of nonsignatory states, again in apparent violation of international law and the Vienna Convention.[15] If a citizen of a nonsignatory state, such as the United States, commits a crime within the court's jurisdiction on the territory of a signatory state, the treaty provides that charges can be brought.[16] This has triggered quite a debate, which will probably not be resolved until a test case comes forward. Nevertheless, provisions such as these demonstrate the broad objectives and determined approach of the new diplomacy treaties.

At the same time, the new diplomacy seeks to expand a second basis of international law: the doctrine of universal jurisdiction. Universal jurisdiction is an old legal doctrine that is being stretched almost beyond recognition. The original justification for allowing courts of any nation to have jurisdiction over certain crimes was that, otherwise, pirates would escape without prosecution, the high seas not being a part of any national jurisdiction. Today, proponents of expansive international law have changed the doctrine from one of locus—the high seas—to one based on the gravity of the offense. The new doctrine of universal jurisdiction is that certain crimes— war crimes, crimes against humanity, genocide—are so serious that any court may take them under its jurisdiction.

The most visible case of modern universal jurisdiction involved the prosecution of General Augusto Pinochet of Chile for violations of human rights law. The courts of both Great Britain and Spain took it upon themselves to pursue this matter, even though his crimes were committed in Chile where, as "senator for life," he enjoyed virtual immunity from prosecution. If the United States is

15. Ibid., art. 34.
16. Rome Statute of International Court, July 17, 1998, art. 12(2).

sometimes considered the world's police force, Belgium apparently aspires to be its courtroom. Belgium's law of universal jurisdiction has been the most aggressive, and cases have been filed there against a wide range of international leaders, from Ariel Sharon to George H. W. Bush, and the leaders of the Rwandan genocide. Recently, Belgium agreed to limit its law to cases involving Belgian nationals, after Donald Rumsfeld suggested that NATO should consider moving its headquarters out of Brussels, rather than risk sending Americans there to face potential arrest based upon Belgian court cases. Nevertheless, this is likely only a temporary setback for universal jurisdiction.

The third prong of the international legal expansion is taking place at the level of international institutions and the campaign for global governance. A 1995 report from the Commission on Global Governance framed much of the agenda.[17] "Our Global Neighborhood" offers comprehensive proposals to "organize life on the planet." From U.N. reform to expansion of the rule of law and the creation of new international organizations and agencies, the suggestions all propose more extensive and assertive global governance. The creation of the ICC was a huge step toward global governance. Even the evolution of the European Union on a regional level creates more of a global governance climate.

Much of the global governance movement is distinctively anti-American in tone and seeks to balance U.S. power. For example, there is considerable interest in the U.N. and elsewhere in sustainable development. The agenda, however, is not just stimulating more activity in underdeveloped countries but encouraging less use of resources by developed countries. A movement against the death penalty is gaining momentum and a U.N. Human Rights Commission rapporteur included the United States on his inspection tour,

17. The Commission on Global Governance, *Our Global Neighborhood* (Oxford University Press, 1995).

which was supposed to focus on "extrajudicial, summary or arbitrary executions." The recent WTO decision finding the U.S. steel tariffs in violation of that organization's policies highlights yet another layer of global governance.

Taken together, there is clearly a significant movement toward the expansion of international law. The new diplomacy has an agenda to expand international controls over human rights, human security, the environment, sustainable development, and the rights of women and children, to name but a few. With new players at the table pursuing strategies through new treaties, through the expansion of universal jurisdiction, and through global governance by international institutions, the game is clearly under way. The effect of all this on the United States must be assessed by policymakers.

International Law Challenges American Values and Interests

The United States should recognize that it has legitimate interests and values it must protect on the international scene. The rapid development of international law—through new treaties, increased use of universal jurisdiction, and expansion of international organizations and global governance—necessarily impinges on the sovereignty and interests of individual nations. Since many of these efforts are motivated by a desire to balance U.S. power, and some are blatantly anti-American in intent, the United States especially must count the cost of expanded international law and weigh that against the public and international relations cost of not participating.

At a very practical level, some expansions of international law expose U.S. citizens to legal and economic risks. The broad jurisdiction of the ICC, for example, poses a real risk of prosecution of U.S. political leaders and military personnel. Although President

Clinton signed the treaty at the last moment, having previously voted against it in Rome, even the Clinton administration acknowledged that the treaty did not contain sufficient protections for American military personnel. With more soldiers abroad than any other nation, the United States faces the greatest risk. Without doubt, the combination of an independent prosecutor, as opposed to charges emanating from the Security Council as was originally intended, and the assertion of the right to charge citizens of non-signatory states creates the opportunity to prosecute American personnel. So, too, has the expansion of universal jurisdiction exposed U.S. political officials to legal processes abroad based on questions of the legitimate exercise of American foreign policy. These are matters to be handled diplomatically, not in a court of law.

Similarly, expansions of treaties in the environmental arena will carry a major economic cost. The proposed limits on global warming in the Kyoto protocols are a first step that carries a huge economic price tag. They will doubtless be followed by even more rigorous restrictions on the use of resources and on manufacturing as the sustainable development agenda moves forward. All nations' leaders owe it to their people to count the cost of such international movements. This is certainly not something the environmental NGOs, with their narrow focus, will do.

A second practical problem with this expansion of international law is that it also intrudes upon domestic policy and values. Jeremy Rabkin provides a wonderful example when he tells of the Nixon administration's and the U.S. Senate's approving the World Heritage Convention in 1972, "a seemingly innocuous treaty under which countries proposed historic or scenic sites for the international equivalent of a landmarks registry."[18] But the big surprise came more than twenty years later when the U.N.'s World Heritage

18. Jeremy Rabkin, *Why Sovereignty Matters* (Washington, D.C.: The AEI Press, 1998): 46–47.

Committee opined that a proposed mining operation near Yellow-
stone National Park, one of the registered sites, would not be appropriate. It took another bill in the House of Representatives,
requiring specific congressional approval for international inspection of U.S. sites, to put that cow back in the barn.

A more current example of international law challenging
domestic values concerns the death penalty. It is difficult to see
how a criminal sentence, arrived at through a judicial system, could
be anything other than a matter of domestic law. Indeed, the death
penalty was not prohibited by the Universal Declaration of Human
Rights in 1948, having just been imposed by the Nuremberg and
Tokyo tribunals. The European Convention on Human Rights,
adopted two years later, recognized a person's right to life, "save
in the execution of a sentence of a court following his conviction
of a crime for which this penalty is provided by law."[19] About one-
half of nations retain capital punishment in some form.

Nevertheless, many human rights activists would like to eliminate the death penalty altogether and would use international law,
if possible, to do so. When a rapporteur from the U.N. Commission
on Human Rights came to the United States to examine capital
punishment, he mentioned that the United Nations was increasingly
moving to a position against the death penalty. One wonders how
that became a part of the United Nations agenda and how, short of
a vote, it could have become an operative concern. Once again,
however, international law may become a platform for influencing
U.S. domestic policy.

Indeed, an agenda is developing that could attempt in a whole
host of areas to replace American values by those decided internationally. A current emphasis on human security, rather than on
national security, could lead to international intervention in previ-

19. Robert F. Drinan, *The Mobilization of Shame* (New Haven, Conn: Yale University Press, 2002): 131.

ously domestic matters. As one commentator noted: "Once security is defined as human security, security policy embraces the totality of state responsibilities for the welfare of citizens from the cradle to the grave."[20] International conferences, to be followed by treaties, continue to develop the rights of women and children in ways that conflict with U.S. law and religious practice. Building on the success of the land mines treaty—which moved that issue from arms control conferences of nations to humanitarian meetings led by NGOs—human rights activists have discussed limits on small arms and even attempts to control the size and scope of the military forces of individual nations.

Moving from the practical to the strategic, the current expansion of international law seeks to move power away from the U.N. Security Council, where the United States can protect its values and interests with its veto power, to other forums and organizations where it is one nation (no matter how small), one vote. Advocates of the ICC freely admit that a primary reason they sought an independent prosecutor, rather than relying on the U.N. Security Council as had been done in the ad hoc tribunals, was to avoid the politics of the permanent members and their veto power. Likewise, the land mines campaign clearly moved its agenda outside of U.N. processes. New diplomacy advocates urge reform of the Security Council, especially expansion of its membership and elimination of the veto, but in the meantime they are eager to move ahead in other forums where U.S. influence can be neutralized and outvoted.

In more conceptual terms, the United States is right to be concerned that the expansion of international law shifts power away from the people and toward more remote, and less democratic, bureaucracies and elites. With its values of grassroots and bottom-up approaches to governance, the United States would not even

20. Ramesh Thakur, "Security in the New Millennium," in Andrew F. Cooper, et al., eds., *Enhancing Global Governance* (Tokyo: United Nations University Press, 2002): 275.

grant its own courts some of the powers accorded the ICC. International organizations rarely incorporate the kinds of political checks and balances or accountability that are at the core of American federalism. Also, the recent appointments of nations known as violators of human rights to important U.N. positions of human rights leadership should remind the United States of the dangers of accountability to international institutions that do not share its democratic values.

In the final analysis the expansion of international law threatens what the United States perhaps values most: its own sovereignty. The basic stance of the globalists is that state sovereignty is an antiquated seventeenth-century concept that will eventually give way to the regional and international institutions that make up the growing web of global governance. They argue that with global communication and markets come global problems that transcend sovereign states and require global solutions. A transition away from state sovereignty and toward global governance is, in the view of the new diplomacy advocates, an evolution to a higher order of things. Those, like the United States, that prize sovereignty are thought to be defending a dinosaur.

Of course sovereign states have been the foundation of the world order at least since the Treaty of Westphalia in 1648. A few new treaties will not change that. But at a deeper level, is state sovereignty an antiquated idea that is simply playing out its string? The case for the continued relevance and usefulness of state sovereignty needs to be reexamined. State sovereignty breaks government down into useful, functional entities that can effectively oversee territories and people. Compared with remote international institutions, state sovereignty brings government closer to the people, a fundamental policy principle that is as relevant today as ever. State sovereignty protects national self-determination and cultural diversity, allowing people to keep historical languages and customs.

Indeed one could argue that some of the most important global agenda items today are better addressed by sovereign states than by international institutions. The problems of terrorism and global security, for example, have only been dealt with when sovereign states took up the challenge. Is anyone really prepared to say that international law and institutions are reaching the point where they are effective in the face of such military and political challenges? Stability requires order, education, and a host of public goods best provided by a sovereign government. Indeed, weakened states generally encourage conflict, as many nations in Africa have learned.

In short, state sovereignty is far from the anachronism some liberal internationalists would have us believe. It has strengths that international institutions would be hard-pressed to develop. If the world is moving down the road toward greater global governance, it is moving slowly, and the movement will need to find a way to respect and incorporate state sovereignty. The rumors of its demise are both premature and overstated. The United States is on the right side of the state sovereignty as opposed to global governance dilemma and should not be blamed or shamed into giving up its position.

Conclusion

Having won the Cold War superpower game, the United States now finds itself at a new diplomatic table with new players and tactics. A new diplomacy, led by NGOs and several small- and medium-sized states, seeks to advance its agenda through the expansion of international law. Although cast in lovely marketing terms such as "soft power," "the rule of law," and "our global neighborhood," the new diplomacy agenda essentially seeks to shift the diplomatic game away from U.S. military and economic strength toward international law and institutions where NGOs, especially, have come to play a leadership role.

At the same time this treaty-based agenda presses forward, globalists seek to expand the legal doctrine of universal jurisdiction and to strengthen the hand of international institutions. Moving away from state sovereignty and toward global governance is clearly the agenda.

Even though the United States has chosen not to sign most of the new diplomacy treaties, American values and interests are nevertheless threatened by this attempt to expand international law. It will not be enough for the United States simply to say "no" to the new diplomacy. The United States will need to energetically engage the new players and tactics, making the case that strong and sovereign states will better meet the needs of the twenty-first century than will wholesale expansions of international law.

—5—

The Dangerous Myth of Universal Jurisdiction

Lee A. Casey and David B. Rivkin Jr.

Introduction

Over the last forty years, activists in the United States, mostly on the left, have used the courts unashamedly to achieve social and political change. This was, perhaps, not surprising in a nation that is largely defined by its constitution and laws, rather than by ethnicity, religion, or race. As early as the 1830s, Alexis de Tocqueville remarked that "[s]carcely any political question arises in the United States that is not resolved, sooner or later, into a judicial question."[1] Nevertheless, the late twentieth century marks a distinct period in American legal history, in which social activists consciously worked to advance a political agenda through litigation, and, in many areas, succeeded. Issues such as abortion, birth control, and public manifestations of religious belief, which before had been dealt with, for good or ill, by elected legislatures, were drawn within the ultimate authority of the courts.

A similar strategy is now being applied on the international

1. Alexis de Tocqueville, *Democracy in America* (Knopf ed. 1951).

level in an effort to achieve substantive policy results (some laudable and some not so laudable) that could not otherwise be obtained through the ordinary political processes of national governments in general, and of the United States in particular. Of course, the tactics are necessarily different from those employed by judicial activists in the United States, since there is no established international court system. The efforts to create such a system, however, are well under way—most notably with the establishment, in July 2002, of an International Criminal Court (ICC) in The Hague. That institution has the authority to investigate, prosecute, and punish the elected leaders of its member states for the criminal offenses defined in its founding statute (the "Rome Statute," having been originally agreed upon at the city of Rome in 1998), including "aggression," war crimes, crimes against humanity, and genocide. In addition, the ICC asserts jurisdiction over the officials and citizens of nonstate-parties in certain circumstances (when the alleged offense took place on the territory of a state-party)—a claim inconsistent with the international law of treaties and repudiated by the United States under both the Clinton and George W. Bush administrations.

Besides making this unprecedented effort to manufacture and impose a "universal" form of jurisdiction on countries that have not ratified the Rome Statute, activists have turned to the principle of "universal jurisdiction" in national courts to achieve their ends. That doctrine—which first appeared as a means of combating piracy in the seventeenth and eighteenth centuries—suggests that any state can define and punish certain "international" criminal offenses, regardless of where the relevant conduct took place or what the nationality of the perpetrators or victims may be. One commentator described the logic of universal jurisdiction as follows: "Since each sovereign power stands in the position of a guardian of international law, and is equally interested in upholding it, any state has the legal right to try war crimes, even though the crimes have been committed against the nationals of another power and in a conflict in which that state is not a party."[2]

From an activist's perspective, the attraction of universality is obvious, particularly in view of concomitant claims (largely based on the Nuremberg Trials following World War II) that government officials enjoy no immunity from prosecution for such offenses. For example, universality would allow a "human rights" lawyer, who opposed the recent war to depose Saddam Hussein, to initiate a criminal prosecution against the American general who commanded that campaign, so long as a cooperative state—in that instance, Belgium—could be found. Although that particular case was dropped, after causing a severe strain on U.S.-Belgian relations and after the consequent repeal of the universality component of Belgium's Law on the Punishment of Serious Violations of International Humanitarian Law, universal jurisdiction remains something like the Holy Grail for international activists, who—without so much as a blush—assert that it is a well established and binding norm of international law. It is, in fact, nothing of the sort.

Although innumerable claims have been made for universal jurisdiction, by activists, academics, and even state officials, even a cursory examination of the actual practice of states—which is what ultimately determines the scope and content of international law—reveals that the doctrine remains an aspiration rather than an established fact. This much is admitted by the most knowledgeable and candid commentators. For example, as Professor Cherif Bassiouni, who was elected as the Chairman of the Drafting Committee of the United Nations Diplomatic Conference on the Establishment of an International Criminal Court, has written:

> Universal jurisdiction is not as well established in conventional and customary international law as its ardent proponents, including major human rights organizations, profess it to be. These

2. Morris Greenspan, *The Modern Law of Land Warfare* 420 (1959).

organizations have listed countries, which they claim rely on universal jurisdiction; in fact, the legal provisions they cite do not stand for that proposition, or at least not as unequivocally as represented.[3]

If universal jurisdiction did exist, one would expect to find dozens of cases, from every corner of the globe, in which the citizens and state officials of one country had been prosecuted and punished by a second country, for offenses on the territory, or against the citizens, of a third. Yet no such body of precedent exists. At most, there are a handful of isolated instances in which universal jurisdiction principles have been cited, although almost never relied upon, by the courts.

Nevertheless, activists continue to invoke the doctrine as a regular aspect of their political or polemical discourse, and many are clearly determined, by any means, to make universal jurisdiction a reality. As a result, the most frequently claimed legal bases for the doctrine of universal jurisdiction, as well as the likely consequences should such a principle become part of international law, deserve examination.

The Enemies of All Mankind

The origins of universal jurisdiction are invariably traced to the law of piracy.[4] At least in Great Britain, claims to a universal criminal jurisdiction over pirates were made as early as the seventeenth century. Pirates, the theory went, were the common enemy of mankind (*hostis humani generis* in Latin), and consequently, all states were lawfully entitled to punish the offense. As British Admiralty

---

3. M. Cherif Bassiouni, "Universal Jurisdiction for International Crimes: Historical Perspectives and Contemporary Practice," 42 *Va. J. Int'l L.* 81, 83 (2001).

4. *See, e.g.,* Ian Brownlie, *Principles of Public International Law* 304–305 (4th ed. 1990).

Judge Sir Charles Hedges famously instructed the grand jury in *Rex v. Dawson*:

> The king of England hath not only an empire and sovereignty over the British seas, but also an undoubted jurisdiction and power, in concurrency with other princes and states, for the punishment of all piracies and robberies at sea, in the most remote parts of the world; so that if any person whatsoever, native or foreigner, Christian or Infidel, Turk or Pagan, with whose country we have no war, with whom we hold trade and correspondence, and are in amity, shall be robbed or spoiled in the Narrow Seas, the Mediterranean, Atlantic, Southern, or any other seas, or the branches thereof, either on this or the other side of the line, it is piracy within the limits of your enquiry, and the cognizance of this court.[5]

However, the extent to which these claims ever evolved into accepted principles of international (as opposed to Anglo-American domestic) law can be, and has been, seriously questioned.

The development of a tangible, as opposed to rhetorical, international law norm supporting universal jurisdiction in piracy cases would have required, as it would for other alleged criminal offenses against international law, a substantial body of precedent in actual state practice. That is, it would require real prosecutions brought by one state against the citizens of another for offenses, otherwise beyond its recognized territorial jurisdiction, against the nationals of a third. This body of law simply does not exist, even with respect to piracy. Indeed, some four years after Sir Charles Hedges charged the jury in *Rex v. Dawson*, King William III took care to inquire whether Louis XIV (with whom he was unusually, and momentarily, at peace), would rather deal with several score of French pirates, who had been captured off the Virginia coast and were

---

5. The Trial of Joseph Dawson, Edward Forseith, William May, William Bishop, James Lewis and John Sparkes, at the Old-Bailey, for Felony and Piracy, 8 William III, A.D. 1696, 13 How. St. Tr. 452, 456 (1816) (hereinafter *Rex v. Dawson*).

then awaiting trial in England. Louis declined, suggesting that such "vermin" were entitled to no favors and that English justice was as good as any.[6] That the question was asked, however, suggests a far more ambivalent state practice than might be supposed from Hedges' assertions, taken in isolation.

As the leading authority on the subject, Professor Alfred Rubin, points out in his magisterial *The Law of Piracy*, since the year 1705 there have been only three cases "of jurisdiction over accused 'pirates' being exercised in the absence of a link to some traditional basis for jurisdiction" other than universal jurisdiction.[7] At most, there was a largely nineteenth-century effort, principally by Great Britain but to a lesser extent by the United States, to use universal jurisdiction claims as a way of justifying claims to police the seas. As explained by Professor Rubin:

> It may be concluded that "universal jurisdiction" when extended beyond the bounds of jurisdiction to prescribe and applied to notions of enforcement and adjudication under national criminal laws, was at best a rule of international law only for a limited period of time [largely in the 19th century] and under political circumstances that no longer apply; at worst, it was merely a hobby horse of Joseph Story and some other learned Americans, and a British attribution to the international legal order of substantive rules forbidding "piracy" and authorizing all nations to apply their municipal laws against it on the high sea, based on a model of imperial Rome, and British racial and commercial ambitions that never did reflect deeper realities, as part of the rationalization of imperialism never really persuasive outside of England and some equally race-proud Europeans and Americans alone.[8]

---

6. *See* Richard Zacks, *The Pirate Hunter* 333 (2002) (citing contemporary diarist Narcissus Luttrell, *A Brief Relation of State Affairs . . . from September 1678 to April 1714* [1857]).

7. Alfred P. Rubin, *The Law of Piracy* 345 (2d ed. 1998).

8. *Id.* at 390–391.

In short, even in the area where it is supposedly best accepted, universal jurisdiction, as an established legal principle, is a phantom.

Moreover, the universal jurisdiction so often claimed for piracy was more narrow by far than the principles asserted for, and necessary to, the broad universality claims made for national universal jurisdiction laws, like those of Belgium or of institutions such as the ICC. In this regard, there were three essential characteristics attributable to the pirates who were said to be the subject of universal jurisdiction. First, they were recognized as individuals who, by their own acts and choice, had put themselves beyond the authority, allegiance, or protection of any state—including and especially their own. Such men sailed against all flags. Second, by definition, pirates acted privately, with the purpose and intent of private gain (*animo furandi*, i.e., with the intent to steal) without the benefit of state authority. They were, by definition, not state actors.[9] Finally, their offenses took place largely beyond the territory (including the territorial sea) of any state.

In these circumstances, a universal authority in states to prescribe the activities of pirates, and to bring them to book when possible, can be maintained more or less consistently with the fundamental principles of the international system—the sovereignty and equality of nation-states. The assertion of jurisdiction over essentially stateless men operating on the high seas does not interfere with the rights of any other sovereign state to protect its nationals or interests. Emphatically, this is not the case for the universality principles claimed by the ICC and its proponents or by the proponents of universal jurisdiction laws like those of Belgium. This form of universality posits the right (and some would even argue the obligation) of states or international institutions both

---

9. Privateers who acted under a commission issued by a sovereign state were not considered "pirates" in law, however much their actual activities may have resembled piracy in practice.

to prescribe certain conduct and to prosecute and adjudicate allegations brought against the nationals of a state, regardless of where the alleged offense may have taken place and of whether the accused was acting under the color of state authority.

The right to prosecute and punish state officials is, of course, a crucial aspect of this universality. The ordinary rule of international law is that government officials are immune from the legal processes of foreign countries because of the fundamental principle that equals cannot judge each other, as described in the maxim *par in parem non habet jurisdictionem*.[10] Universal jurisdiction posits that government officials are not only subject to the relevant substantive legal norms but also that they can be prosecuted for violating those norms, even if the violation took place in the execution of their official duties and even if it was otherwise consistent with the constitution and laws of their own country. The Nuremberg Trials, through which the surviving Nazi leadership was punished after World War II, are usually cited in support of this principle— as it happens, incorrectly.

The Nuremberg Legacy

When the twentieth century began, the city of Nuremberg had a long and honored history. An independent, prosperous, and politically important town during the Middle Ages (joined to the neighboring kingdom of Bavaria only during the Napoleonic wars), it was a favorite of nineteenth-century German romantics, including Richard Wagner, who wrote "Die Meistersinger" in the city's honor. Unfortunately, Nuremberg's rich history also attracted one

---

10. *See* Brownlie, *supra* note 4, at 324. As Professor Brownlie also notes, governmental immunity also is based on the principle of "non-intervention in the internal affairs of other states." Both of these principles were restated in Article 2 of the United Nations Charter. *See* U.N. Charter, Ch. I, Art. 2, reprinted in Ian Brownlie, *Basic Documents in International Law* 1, 3 (4th ed. 1995).

particularly zealous, and infamous, Wagner fan—Adolph Hitler—who used the city as something of an unofficial capital for the Nazi Party. It was here that the massive party rallies of the 1930s took place and that the odious "Nuremberg Laws," depriving Germany's Jews of citizenship and civil rights, were promulgated. Also an armaments manufacturing center, Nuremberg was 90 percent destroyed by Allied bombing during World War II. Its close connection to Nazi pageantry and its location in the American occupation zone made Nuremberg an obvious choice for the trials by which it is best known today.

The Nuremberg Trials—actually the proceedings of the International Military Tribunal (IMT) which convened in the city's only partly destroyed "palais de justice" from 1945 to 1946—are often cited, certainly by casual commentators and sometimes even by courts, as the foundation of modern "universal" jurisdiction.[11] Nothing, however, could be further from the truth. Despite the efforts by many proponents of universality to use the Nuremberg Trials as a precedent for that principle, both in practice and theory the IMT's authority was far less sweeping. It never claimed to act under the principles of universal jurisdiction but represented an ad hoc institution created by the victorious Allies to punish men who could not be permitted to go free.

Like much during and after World War II, the Nuremberg Trials were the result of a compromise. Winston Churchill wanted simply to shoot the defeated Nazi leadership—within six hours of capture, after proper identification.[12] This became the principal position of the British government, which maintained that, although "[l]esser war criminals might be tried within the limits of established law on war crimes . . . a Hitler trial would require new laws to be made up to match the crimes, and this was not only legally

11. *See Demjanjuk v. Petrovsky*, 776 F.2d 571, 582 (6th Cir. 1985).
12. Richard Overy, *Interrogations: The Nazi Elite in Allied Hands, 1945* 6–7 (2001).

dubious, but would give the defence endless opportunities to argue so."[13]

Ironically, it was the Soviet Union that insisted most strongly on a "trial." From Stalin's perspective, it would be the grandest of his show trials,[14] an open statement to the world of Communism's triumph over National Socialism, and of his personal triumph over Hitler. The Roosevelt administration was divided, with Secretary of the Treasury Henry Morganthau Jr. supporting Churchill's view, and Secretary of War Henry Stimson arguing for due process of law consistent with the Bill of Rights. Ultimately, the matter was in Stimson's portfolio, and he prevailed, relying, as one author notes, "on a strange alliance with a Soviet system almost entirely at odds with American conceptions of justice."[15]

With both the United States and the Soviet Union, for their very different reasons, insisting on a trial, the British Government acceded—perhaps not coincidentally after Hitler committed suicide, since giving the fallen dictator yet another "platform" was one of Churchill's principal objections to a trial. However, the fundamental legal issues pointed out by the British remained. Although there was a long and accessible tradition for punishing violations of the laws and customs of war, there was no obvious legal basis for reaching beyond the Third Reich's military leadership into the Nazi Party hierarchy itself. Limiting postwar justice to the German high command would have pulled in a number of the chief surviving culprits, including Hermann Goering, but would not have reached men such as Albert Speer, Hitler's armament minister, Joachim von Ribbentrop, Hitler's foreign minister, and Robert Ley, head of the Nazi "labor front" who, along with Speer, oversaw one of the most brutal and widespread forced-labor systems in history.

As the British government anticipated, the Nuremberg defen-

13. *Id.* at 7.
14. *Id.* at 8.
15. *Id.* at 10.

dants challenged the IMT's authority, as well as the legality of charges, particularly "crimes against peace," that had not been recognized as criminal offenses before the war. In response to the first claim, the court did not rely on some generalized legal authority inherent in the "international community," nor did it cite principles of "universal jurisdiction." Instead, it openly and unequivocally relied on the rights of Germany's conquerors to legislate for that defeated state. In this regard, the court noted as follows:

> The jurisdiction of the Tribunal is defined in the Agreement and Charter, and the crimes coming within the jurisdiction of the Tribunal, for which there shall be individual responsibility, are set out in Article 6. The law of the Charter is decisive, and binding upon the Tribunal.
>
> The making of the Charter was the exercise of the sovereign legislative power by the countries to which the German Reich unconditionally surrendered; and the undoubted right of these countries to legislate for the occupied territories has been recognized by the civilized world.[16]

Indeed, the authority of the Nuremberg Trials as precedent for any legal proposition is doubtful. The two most important "innovations" claimed for the IMT were the principles, stated in Article 6 and 7 of its Charter, that individuals could be tried and punished for criminal offenses against international law, even though those offenses had not also been properly enacted into national legal codes and regardless of the immunity traditionally recognized for high government officials. Neither has been borne out in the ensuing years by actual state practice.

The most controversial aspect of the Nuremberg Trials was the arraignment of individuals on a charge of waging, and conspiring to wage, an aggressive war. This charge did not exist in the German criminal code before the war, nor did it figure in the criminal codes

16. *The Nurnberg Trial*, 6 F.R.D. 69, 107.

of the other Great Powers. To justify the charge against the Nazis, the IMT cited the Kellogg-Briand Pact of 1928, under which the parties (including Germany and the Allied powers), had renounced war as an instrument of policy. This treaty, however, had none of the normal characteristics of criminal law, such as a definition of the elements of the "offense" or an established range of punishments.[17]

In response to the claim that the charge would violate the maxim *nullum crimen sine lege* (no crime without a law), the tribunal first noted that it was not bound by such principles: "The law of the Charter is decisive, and binding upon the Tribunal. . . . The Charter makes the planning or waging of a war of aggression or a war in violation of international treaties a crime; and it is therefore not strictly necessary to consider whether and to what extent aggressive war was a crime before the execution of the London Agreement."[18] This was obviously a strange claim to make for a tribunal then engaged in trying individuals for having themselves recognized no authority higher than their own will, but, nevertheless, it was the actual "holding" of the court. In addition, the court noted that this rule, which is enshrined in the United States Constitution as the injunction against expost facto laws, is on the international level simply a "general principle of justice" and not an actual "limitation on sovereignty."[19]

Second, the IMT ruled that individual state officials could not

17. When faced with this undeniable fact, the IMT merely suggested that the Hague Convention, which codified many of the offenses most commonly known as "war crimes," such as the mistreatment of prisoners of war and the misuse of flags of truce, also did not contain specific criminal charges. *Id.* at 108. Of course, these offenses were based on long-standing state practice, and already were specifically accepted as criminal acts in at least some of the military codes extant at the time. This simply was not the case for "waging aggressive war."

18. *Id.* at 107.

19. *Id.* This was a significant observation on the IMT's part, effectively emphasizing its character as a tribunal established as an exercise of the German sovereignty, then held by the Allies, rather than as a body established under international law.

claim "immunity." In this regard, the court noted: "He who violates the laws of war cannot obtain immunity while acting in pursuance of the authority of the state if the state authorizing action moves outside its competence under International law."[20] It further noted: "The provisions of this article are in conformity with the law of all nations. That a soldier was ordered to kill or torture in violation of the international law of war has never been recognized as a defense to such act of brutality, though, as the Charter here provides, the order may be urged in mitigation of the punishment."[21]

This reasoning, of course, merely suggests that government officials are not above the law and that their actions may constitute criminal violations. It does not answer the far more difficult question of under what circumstances, and by what authority, a government official may be tried and punished for such violations. The International Court of Justice (ICJ) noted this important distinction in its 2002 opinion in *Congo v. Belgium*.[22] As will be discussed below in detail, that case involved an assertion of universal jurisdiction by Belgium against the Congolese foreign minister, who was accused of war crimes and crimes against humanity in the Congo. After examining state practice in this area, the court concluded that the Congolese foreign minister was immune from Belgium's criminal jurisdiction. It noted, however:

> The *immunity* from jurisdiction enjoyed by incumbent Ministers for Foreign Affairs does not mean that they enjoy *impunity* in respect of any crimes they might have committed, irrespective of their gravity. Immunity from criminal jurisdiction and individual criminal responsibility are quite separate concepts. . . .
> Accordingly, the immunities enjoyed under international law

20. *Id.* at 110.
21. *Id.* at 111.
22. Case Concerning the Arrest Warrant of Apr. 11, 2000 *(Democratic Republic of the Congo v. Belgium),* 41 I.L.M. 536 (I.C.J. Feb. 14, 2002), at International Court of Justice, http://www.icj-cij.org/icjwww/idochat/icobejudgment/icobe_ijudgment_20020214.pdf.

by an incumbent or former Minister of Foreign Affairs do not represent a bar to criminal prosecution in certain circumstances.

First, such persons enjoy no criminal immunity under international law in their own countries, and may thus be tried by those countries' courts in accordance with the relevant rules of domestic law.

Secondly, they will cease to enjoy immunity from foreign jurisdiction if the State which they represent or have represented decides to waive that immunity.[23]

And, in fact, the ultimate basis of the IMT's refusal to recognize any immunity for the accused Nazis was very much in accord with these principles.

As noted above, the IMT justified itself with reference to its Charter. Article 7 of that Charter stated plainly that "[t]he official position of defendants, whether as heads of state, or responsible officials in government departments, shall not be considered as freeing them from responsibility, or mitigating punishment."[24] The Charter, as the court also stated, was lawful as an exercise of the Allies' "undoubted right . . . recognized by the civilized world" to legislate for a defeated Germany. It was an exercise of German sovereignty and, as a consequence, whatever immunity the Nuremberg defendants might have been entitled to claim in a foreign court, they could assert no such immunity before the IMT.[25] Stated

23. *Id.* at par. 60–61.
24. 6 F.R.D. at 110.
25. Like Germany, Japan also surrendered unconditionally in 1945. A tribunal, sitting in Tokyo, was established to try war crimes offenses in the Far East. The charter of this court was adopted by General Douglas McArthur in his capacity as the Supreme Commander for the Allied Powers in Japan, under authority acknowledged in the Japanese Instrument of Surrender, dated September 2, 1945. This document indicated the assent of the Japanese emperor and government to the Potsdam Declaration (July 26, 1945), which made clear that war criminals would be punished. The Potsdam Declaration was made by the United States, Great Britain, and the Nationalist Government of China and stated: "[w]e do not intend that the Japanese shall be enslaved as a race or destroyed as a nation, but stern justice shall be meted out to all war criminals, including those who have visited cruelties upon our prisoners."

differently, because their immunity as state officials under international law belonged to the German state, and not to the individual defendants themselves, that immunity could be, and was, lawfully waived by the Allies who were then exercising Germany's sovereignty.

The Trial of Adolph Eichmann

The IMT, of course, did not try all the top Nazis. A number of the men who were the most important cogs in Hitler's murder machine escaped after the war, many to South America. The most notorious and culpable of these was Adolph Eichmann. His prosecution and execution by Israel may well be the only instance in which a truly universal jurisdiction was exercised over the offenses—war crimes, crimes against humanity, and genocide—for which that jurisdiction is most often asserted by its proponents. It was, however, by no means a clear case.

Although reared in Austria, Eichmann was German by birth and trained for a time at least as an engineer; however, he was working as a traveling salesman when he joined the Nazi Party in 1932. By 1934 Eichmann had joined Heinrich Himmler's SS and was working in Berlin as an SD (SS security service) official with expertise in "Jewish issues." In 1939 he became head of the RSHA (Reich Main Security Office) section dealing with Jewish "evacuation" and "resettlement" (euphemisms for deportation and murder) under the authority of Reinhard Heydrich (known, before he was successfully targeted by British-backed Czech partisans, as the Butcher of Prague, or Hangman Heydrich). In that capacity, Eichmann attended the 1942 Wansee Conference at which the extermination of Europe's Jews was mapped out. He was, in short, the official responsible for the day-to-day implementation of the Final Solution.

For fifteen years after Germany's defeat, Eichmann remained

one of the world's most wanted men. Israeli agents finally located him in Argentina, and on May 11, 1960, he was seized by the Israeli Secret Service and taken to trial in Israel. There, he was charged under the Nazis and Nazi Collaborators (Punishment) Law, and his case presented the Israeli courts with a substantial problem of jurisdiction. All Eichmann's offenses had been committed in the territory of countries other than Israel, against citizens of countries other than Israel, at a time when Israel did not exist. In other words, under the normal rules governing the exercise of judicial authority, national and international, the state of Israel had no right to try Adolph Eichmann who was not an Israeli national.

In addressing this question both the Israeli trial court and the Israeli Supreme Court on appeal referred to principles of universal jurisdiction. There was little question that, as the courts observed, Eichmann's offenses had been universally condemned or that, as the Israeli Supreme Court noted, "their harmful and murderous effects were so embracing and widespread as to shake the international community to its very foundations."[26] However, neither the trial court nor the Israeli Supreme Court was content to rest its decision on universal jurisdiction. Like the IMT at Nuremberg, the courts' actual holdings rested on the relevant statutory authority, rather than on international law. In this respect, both courts ruled inadmissible the argument, raised by Eichmann's lawyers, that the Nazis and Nazi Collaborators (Punishment) Law was inconsistent with international law because "it conflict[ed] . . . with the principle of territorial sovereignty, which postulates that only the country within whose territory the offense was committed or to which the offender belongs—in this case Germany—has the right to punish therefore."[27] Both courts concluded that they were bound to apply that law whether or not it was inconsistent with international law principles. The Israeli Supreme Court noted that

26. *Eichmann Case*, 36 I.L.R. 1, 304 (1968) [hereinafter *Eichmann Case*].
27. *Id.* at 279.

where such a conflict [between international and municipal law] does exist, it is the duty of the Court to give preference to and apply the laws of the local Legislature . . . True, the presumption must be that the Legislature strives to adjust its laws to the principles of international law which have received general recognition. But where a contrary intention clearly emerges from the statute itself, that presumption loses its force and the Court is enjoined to disregard it.[28]

In other words, whatever the correct answer under international law might be, the courts of Israel were bound to apply the municipal law of Israel as enacted by the Knesset, and arguments suggesting that the law was beyond the Knesset's authority under international law were inherently insufficient to defeat the courts' jurisdiction.

Moreover, even in the courts' dicta, discussing universality at great length, neither body was content to rest on universal jurisdiction alone. Both also invoked the somewhat less controversial "protective" principle, as well as ideas of passive personality jurisdiction.[29] Here, the trial court reasoned that

[i]f an effective link (not necessarily an identity) existed between the State of Israel and the Jewish people, then a crime intended to exterminate the Jewish people has an indubitable connection with the State of Israel [presumably sufficient to justify protective jurisdiction].

The connection between the State of Israel and the Jewish

---

28. *Id.* at 280–281.

29. Under the "protective" principle of international criminal jurisdiction, states assert jurisdiction over individuals acting abroad to attack or undercut the state's security. As noted by Professor Brownlie, "[n]early all states assume jurisdiction over aliens for acts done abroad which affect the security of the state, a concept which takes in a variety of political offenses, but is not necessarily confined to political acts." Brownlie, *supra* note 4, at 304. The "passive personality" principle permits a state to punish acts beyond its territory that harm its own nationals. Although there is more state practice supporting these forms of jurisdiction than universality, common law jurisdictions have been dubious of both, preferring the relative certainties of territorial jurisdiction. *See generally, id.* at 303–304.

people needs no explanation. The State of Israel was established and recognized as the State of the Jews.[30]

On this point, the Israeli Supreme Court noted that "we fully agree with every word said by the [trial] Court on this subject."[31]

Thus, the actual metes and bounds of the Eichmann decision severely undercut its value as a precedent for universal jurisdiction. That value is further reduced because Germany appears, at least tacitly, to have consented to Eichmann's prosecution in Israel. As noted above, the decisive test of the universal jurisdiction principle is not the assertion of power by one or more states but its vindication over the objections of the defendant's own state of citizenship. Eichmann was a German national, at least at the time his offenses were committed. Germany, however, chose neither to contest his prosecution nor to champion his case. In fact, Germany's refusal to assert authority over Eichmann (by rejecting his demand to be extradited to the Federal Republic of Germany for trial), or otherwise to intervene, was noted as significant by the Israeli Supreme Court in its conclusion that his trial in Israel would not violate the territoriality principle of international law.[32]

30. *Eichmann Case, supra* note 26, at 52.
31. *Id.* at 304.
32. *Id.* at 287. Argentina also did not champion Eichmann because of his "nationality," although it did strenuously object to his seizure by Israeli agents on its territory. Ultimately, this issue was worked out diplomatically between the two nations. *Id.* at 5–7.

In another case involving Israel's Nazis and Nazi Collaborators (Punishment) Law, the United States Court of Appeals for the Sixth Circuit also accepted universal jurisdiction as an established fact—largely based on claims made in the Restatement (Third) of the Foreign Relations Law of the United States, rather than on any effort to examine the actual practice of states. *See Demjanjuk v. Petrovsky*, 776 F. 2d 571, 579–583 (6th Cir. 1985). This case was, in fact, not a criminal prosecution but involved the extradition, to Israel, of a man accused of having been an especially brutal guard ("Ivan the Terrible") at the Treblinka death camp. The court concluded that he was accused of offenses within Israel's jurisdiction based on the universality principle and duly certified his extradition. The Israeli courts ultimately concluded that Demjanjuk had not been proven to be Ivan the Terrible, and acquitted.

The Attempted Extradition of Augusto Pinochet

Besides the Eichmann case, the effort by Spanish investigating magistrate Balthazar Garzon to extradite, for trial in Spain, former Chilean dictator Augusto Pinochet is also usually cited as support for universal jurisdiction. As an instance of state practice, however, the Pinochet case stands for just the opposite proposition.

Augusto Pinochet Ugarte seized power in 1973, deposing Chile's leftist government, led by Salvador Allende. At the time, Pinochet was commander-in-chief of Chile's armed forces. He was named president in 1974, after having shut down Chile's parliament. He finally surrendered power in 1990, when a democratic government was elected, although he remained as military commander-in-chief until 1998. He then became a "senator for life" and effectively enjoyed immunity from prosecution in Chile. He remains a highly controversial figure in Chile and elsewhere.

There is little doubt that, during Pinochet's dictatorship, the Chilean government engaged in torture, murder, and other forms of political repression on a large scale. In addition, a portion of Pinochet's rule corresponded to years of military dictatorship in neighboring Argentina, including the so-called Dirty War from 1976 to 1983—in which he allegedly cooperated. Thousands of people disappeared during the Dirty War, in an effort by the Argentine military to eliminate left-wing dissent. Some were thrown out of aircraft flying over the South Atlantic Ocean. Although the Argentine military junta relinquished power in 1983, after its humiliating defeat by Great Britain in the Falklands War, a general amnesty was granted in 1991, at a time when Argentina's president feared a new military coup.

Beginning in the 1990s Balthasar Garzon, an investigating magistrate working for Spain's highest criminal court, the National Court, initiated an investigation into Argentina's Dirty War—in which a number of Spanish citizens had been killed. Garzon, a socialist who has served as a junior minister in the Spanish government, first made his name pursuing Basque separatists. His Argentine investigation led him to Pinochet's role in the so-called Operation Condor, a program under which various South American security services, including those of Chile and Argentina, cooperated to eliminate left-wing opponents. (One target of Operation Condor was Orlando Letelier, former Chilean ambassador to the United States, who was murdered in Washington, D.C., in 1976.)

When Pinochet traveled to Britain in 1998 seeking medical treatment, Garzon issued an international arrest warrant and a request for extradition. This led to a seventeen-month drama, during which Pinochet was held under house arrest in Britain while his ultimate fate was debated in the courts. In the end, his case was heard by the House of Lords, which ruled that he could be extradited to Spain. As in previous supposed universal jurisdiction cases, however, that doctrine was not the basis of the court's decision. Although a number of the judges discussed universal jurisdiction in their opinions and even concluded that it was an accepted principle of international law, like the Israeli Supreme Court in the Eichmann case, they looked to national law—and to the law of treaties—for a rule of decision.

In this regard, a majority of the lords reached two conclusions. First, Pinochet could be extradited from Britain but only for offenses cognizable under legislation passed to implement the International Convention against Torture and Other Cruel, Inhuman, or Degrading Treatment or Punishment of 1984 ("Torture Convention"), that is, after September 29, 1988. Second, Pinochet could not claim immunity from prosecution for offenses alleged to have taken place after that date because the Torture Convention implied a waiver of such immunity, or because, after the convention's effective date, torture was no longer viewed as an official act covered by immunity.[33]

The fundamental linkage to the Torture Convention is, of course, highly significant. Although more than one of the judges suggested that torture constituted an international crime well before the Torture Convention took effect, the panel nevertheless concluded that Pinochet was extraditable to Spain *only* for offenses after that time. Thus, to the extent that there was a "universal" jurisdiction in this case, it was based on a treaty—to which both Britain and Chile were parties—and not on a customary international law that would, or could, bind nonparties. In such instances, all treaty parties are, at least in theory, permitted to enforce the treaty's terms. This, however, is based on the consent of the relevant states, and not on some legal or judicial authority otherwise inherent in the international community as a whole. Moreover, even with respect to these instruments, there is little state practice actually supporting the right of an otherwise uninvolved state-party to take judicial action against the citizens or officials of another state-party for violations against a third, with the targeted state accepting its right to do so. If, as universal jurisdiction proponents claim, the doctrine is so very well established, there should be many such cases.

In the end, however, even the Pinochet matter did not provide such an example. Chile strongly objected to Spain's efforts to extradite Pinochet and, after all of the legal wrangling was over, with the House of Lords concluding that Pinochet was subject to extradition, the British government still did not consider itself *legally compelled* to make the transfer. The responsible official, British Secretary of State for Home Affairs Jack Straw, acknowl-

---

33. *R. v. Bow Street Magistrates*, 1 App. Cas. 147, 2 All Eng. Rep. 97 (1999).

edged his own belief that "universal jurisdiction against persons charged with international crimes should be effective" but nevertheless concluded that Pinochet was medically unfit to stand trial, and released him.[34] This was, of course, a diplomatic rather than a legal solution. Shortly after his release, Pinochet was awarded legal costs of £500,000, paid by the British taxpayer.[35]

Belgian Weltmacht

In setting Pinochet at liberty in March 2000, Secretary Straw also declined to extradite him to at least three other European states, France, Switzerland, and Belgium, which had made requests similar to that of Spain.[36] The last, Belgium, has clearly been the most aggressive universal jurisdiction aspirant in the past decade, and the rise, decline, and fall of its universal jurisdiction law reveals, perhaps better than anything else, how dubious and flawed is the universal jurisdiction doctrine.

Belgium's Law of June 16, 1993, on the Punishment of Serious Violations of International Humanitarian Law, as amended in 1999, purported to vest jurisdiction in the Belgian courts over a series of international criminal offenses (including war crimes), regardless of the nationality of the defendants, the victims, or where the offenses took place. The law also provided that official governmental immunity "shall not prevent the application of the present Law."[37] Before the 2003 Iraq war, when the law was finally invoked against the United States, its most spectacular application

34. *See* Statement of Secretary of State for the Home Department to the House of Commons (Mar. 2, 2000), at http://www.publications.parliament.uk/pa/cm199900/cmhansrd/vo000302/debtext/00302-10.htm#00302-10_spmin0.

35. *See* BBC News, "Pinochet Wins Legal Costs" (Mar. 6, 2000), at http://news.bbc.co.uk/2/hi/uk_news/667982.stm.

36. *See* Home Office, *Extradition Proceedings Against Senator Pinochet* (Sept. 12, 2000), at http://www.homeoffice.gov.uk/docs/pinochet.html.

37. *See Congo v. Belgium, supra* note 22, at 9.

was against the Democratic Republic of the Congo's foreign minister, Abdulaye Yerodia Ndombasi. Because of allegations forwarded by a number of private citizens, an international arrest warrant was issued for this man, to which his government took the gravest exception. As noted above, the Congo challenged Belgium's jurisdictional claims, as well as its right to initiate prosecutions against foreign government officials, in the ICJ. On the question of universal jurisdiction, its Application noted that Belgium's law was in "[v]iolation of the principle that a State may not exercise its authority on the territory of another State and of the principle of sovereign equality among all Members of the United Nations, as laid down in Article 2, paragraph 1, of the Charter of the United Nations."[38]

The ICJ chose not to address the universal jurisdiction question so presented but ruled instead that Belgium's arrest warrant violated international law by ignoring the well-settled immunity of high-level government officials from criminal prosecution while in office. This ruling, however, was significant in and of itself, since this rule of immunity had been considered by many to have been fatally undercut across the board by the Nuremberg and Tokyo tribunal trials. In that regard, the ICJ stated, citing both national efforts to prosecute foreign officials and the Nuremberg and Tokyo military tribunals:

> The Court has carefully examined State practice, including national legislation and those few decisions of national higher courts, such as the House of Lords or the French Court of Cassation. It has been unable to deduce from this practice that there exists under customary international law any form of exception to the rule according immunity from criminal jurisdiction and inviolability to incumbent Ministers of Foreign Affairs, where they are suspected of having committed war crimes or crimes against humanity.

38. *Id.*

The Court has also examined the rules concerning the immunity or criminal responsibility of persons having an official capacity contained in the legal instruments creating international criminal tribunals [including the Nuremberg, Tokyo, and U.N. ad hoc tribunals for the former Yugoslavia and Rwanda]. It finds that these rules likewise do not enable it to conclude that any such exception exists in customary international law in regard to national courts.[39]

Despite this rebuke, Belgium's efforts to impose its own version of worldwide justice continued. By the spring of 2003, more than two dozen allegations had been lodged under its universal jurisdiction law, including complaints against Israeli Prime Minister Ariel Sharon, former President George H. W. Bush, former Secretary of Defense and current Vice President Dick Cheney, Secretary of State Colin Powell, and General Tommy Franks, all related to the 1991 or 2003 Iraqi wars.

Visiting Brussels in June 2003, Secretary of Defense Donald Rumsfeld delivered a blunt message. United States officials could not be expected to travel to a country where they might be the target of frivolous, politically motivated charges. American support for the continuing presence of NATO headquarters in Belgium, he made clear, was at issue. With this, Belgium backed off. The law had, in fact, been turned against its own foreign minister, Louis Michel, who was accused of international violations because of an arms sale to Nepal. In August 2003 the law was amended to restrict its reach to cases involving Belgian nationals or residents as perpetrators or victims.[40]

Although the checkered history of Belgium's "universal jurisdiction" law presents more than a few elements of the theater of the absurd, from an international law perspective, its rise and fall

39. *Id.* at 21.
40. Glenn Frankel, "Belgian War Crimes Law Undone by Its Reach," *Wash. Post*, A1 (Sept. 30, 2002).

are highly significant. As suggested above, international law is first and foremost a form of customary law, and it is made by state practice. With Belgium's retreat—in the face of serious objections from the accused persons' own countries—the whole concept of universal jurisdiction was dealt a serious, and well-deserved, blow. As a Belgian senator who supported the law correctly noted of its revision, "[w]e didn't lose everything, but we lost a lot. . . . we moved backward rather than forward."[41]

Poor Relations:
The Alien Tort Claims Act

The United States' Alien Tort Claims Act (ATCA) is sometimes also cited as an example of the exercise of universal jurisdiction.[42] In fact, there are important distinctions between efforts to invoke a universal criminal jurisdiction, permitting any state to prosecute and punish the citizens and officials of any other state for international "offenses," and efforts to sue government officials in tort for alleged violations of international law. First, of course, is the criminal nature of one kind of proceeding, and the civil nature of the other. Second, the Supreme Court has made clear that the ATCA is subject to the constraints of foreign sovereign immunities, as recognized in the United States under the Foreign Sovereign Immunities Act of 1976 (FSIA).[43] In addition, while universal criminal jurisdiction suggests that authority can be exercised over an accused anywhere in the world, through an international arrest warrant, the ATCA can be invoked only if the defendant can be found in the United States itself. Nevertheless, to the extent that the courts of the United States have, in a handful of cases, adjudicated claims for tortious violations of international law, the

41. *Id.*
42. 28 U.S.C. sec. 1350.
43. 28 U.S.C. secs. 1602–1611.

ATCA raises many of the same policy concerns as does criminal universal jurisdiction.

The Forgotten Statute

The ATCA is nothing if not an enigma. Enacted as part of the Judiciary Act of 1789 (which established the federal court system in accordance with the newly adopted United States Constitution), its purpose and meaning are utterly obscure. The law provides that "[t]he district courts shall have original jurisdiction of any civil action by an alien for a tort only, committed in violation of the law of nations or a treaty of the United States."[44] No legislative history dealing with the provision has been found, and before 2004 it had never been construed by the United States Supreme Court. For nearly two hundred years after the ATCA became law, it was effectively dormant. In 1980, however, the family of a murdered Paraguayan youth invoked the law to sue his alleged killer, a former Paraguayan police official, in a New York federal court. The victim had been tortured. All the parties were citizens of Paraguay, but all were in the United States at the time the action was brought.

Although the trial court dismissed the case for lack of jurisdiction, in *Filartiga v. Pena*,[45] the United States Court of Appeals for the Second Circuit reversed, concluding that the suit could be maintained under the ATCA. The judges reasoned that the general injunction against state-sponsored torture had become so widely accepted that the court could properly conclude that "official torture is now prohibited by the law of nations."[46] The court failed, however, to identify a specific cause of action that would permit a tort claim to be based on official torture and suggested that the law of Paraguay might well apply to the case. The court dealt with the

44. 28 U.S.C. sec. 1350.
45. 630 F. 2d 876 (2d Cir. 1980).
46. *Id.* at 884.

question of the United States' right to adjudicate the case as follows:

> Common law courts of general jurisdiction regularly adjudicate transitory tort claims between individuals over whom they exercise personal jurisdiction, wherever the tort occurred. . . .
>
> It is not extraordinary for a court to adjudicate a tort claim arising outside of its territorial jurisdiction. A state or nation has a legitimate interest in the orderly resolution of disputes among those within its borders, and where the lex loci delicti commissi is applied, it is an expression of comity to give effect to the laws of the state where the wrong occurred. . . .
>
> . . . Here, where in personum jurisdiction has been obtained over the defendant, the parties agree that the acts alleged would violate Paraguayan law, and the policies of the forum are consistent with the foreign law, state court jurisdiction would be proper. Indeed, appellees conceded as much at oral argument.[47]

The court further concluded that the federal courts could properly hear such a claim in light of the Constitution's limitation on federal court jurisdiction, because the law of nations was considered part of "federal common law."

Four years later, in *Tel-Oren v. Libya*, the United States Court of Appeals for the District of Columbia Circuit also addressed the ATCA.[48] In that case, a group of mostly Israeli citizens sought damages from Libya, the Palestine Liberation Organization (PLO), and various affiliated groups, arising out of a 1978 terrorist attack on an Israeli civilian bus. The trial court had dismissed the action, concluding that it lacked subject matter jurisdiction.

A three-judge panel of the District of Columbia Circuit affirmed that decision but suggested three separate reasons for so doing. Judge Harry Edwards accepted the reasoning of the court in *Filartiga*, but concluded that it was inapplicable to this case since

47. *Id.* at 885.
48. 726 F. 2d 774 (D.C. Cir. 1984).

the principal defendants, that is, the PLO, were private individuals rather than state actors. He discerned no right under international law to be free of attacks by private individuals in the circumstances presented. Judge Robert H. Bork rejected the reasoning in *Filartiga*, correctly noting that the Second Circuit had distinctly failed to identify any actual cause of action, recognized by international law, that could be enforced in a suit under the ATCA. He concluded that the court should not imply such an action in an area, foreign affairs, otherwise committed by the Constitution to the political branches. Finally, Judge Roger Robb agreed that the case must be dismissed, but because the entire area presented a political question, involving American foreign policy and "standards that defy judicial application." The matter was, in short, nonjusticiable in the first instance. The result, as Judge Bork stated at the close of his opinion, was that "it is impossible to say even what the law of this circuit is" with respect to the ATCA.[49]

Rights as Opposed to Rights of Action

The situation improved little in the twenty years after *Tel-Oren* was decided—although an increasing number of ATCA cases were brought, some attempting to expand the statute beyond the limits suggested by Judge Edwards, to reach private entities.[50] The Supreme Court first addressed the ATCA, albeit tangentially, in

49. *Id.* at 823. Congress, at least, took Judge Bork's criticisms seriously and later passed the Torture Victims Protection Act, Pub. L. No. 102-256, 106 Stat. 73, in 1992. This statute does create a cause of action for official torture and its detailed provisions are an excellent example of the elements that, in other areas, the courts would be required to improvise. In addition, and significantly, Congress imposed a requirement that the plaintiff have exhausted "adequate and available remedies in the place in which the conduct giving rise to the claim occurred."

50. *See, e.g., Kadic v. Karadzic*, 70 F.3d 232 (2d Cir. 1995) (jurisdiction found under ATCA over claim against leader of Bosnian Serb faction); *Doe v. Unocal Corp.*, 963 F. Supp. 880 (C.D. Cal. 1997) (suit against oil company allegedly involved in state-sponsored human rights violations in Burma).

Argentine Republic v. Amerada Hess Shipping Corp.,[51] in which it made clear that actions brought under the ATCA are subject to the requirements of the FSIA.[52]

In that case, the owner and lessee of an oil tanker sued the Argentine government for damage done to the vessel during the 1982 Falklands War between Argentina and Great Britain. The ship had been attacked by Argentine forces and, as a result, later had to be scuttled. The Supreme Court held that the action, which had been brought under the ATCA, as well as the general admiralty and maritime jurisdiction of the United States and "universal jurisdiction," was properly dismissed because the FSIA provided Argentina immunity in these circumstances.

Significantly, however, in rejecting the plaintiff's claim that various international agreements, binding on both Argentina and the United States, created an exception to the FSIA in this instance, the Court emphasized the critical distinction between a substantive violation and the right to sue. It noted that there is an exception to the FSIA's general recognition of foreign state sovereign immunity, in which the law's provisions would "expressly conflict" with an international agreement to which the United States was a party when the statute was enacted. The Court went on to point out, however, that the relevant conventions in this case "only set forth substantive rules of conduct and state that compensation shall be paid for certain wrongs. They do not create private rights of action for foreign corporations to recover compensation from foreign states in United States courts."[53]

This, of course, was the critical problem, correctly identified by Judge Bork in *Tel-Oren*, with the Second Circuit's analysis in *Filartiga*, and with theories of universal jurisdiction generally. Although the ATCA permits the federal courts to hear cases for

51. 488 U.S. 428 (1980).
52. 28 U.S.C. secs. 1602–1611.
53. 488 U.S. at 442.

torts "in violation of the law of nations or a treaty of the United States," it does not create or identify any specific cause of action, such as battery or negligence in domestic tort law, on which a private plaintiff can actually sue. That is, the law does not set forth the circumstances in which an injured alien would be entitled to a judgment in court—specifying what substantive elements (the offensive or impermissible conduct, level of intent, and kind of physical or mental harm) he or she must prove in order to recover. Similarly, it does not set forth the burden of proof the plaintiff must carry. Must the plaintiff prove the necessary elements by a preponderance of the evidence, by clear and convincing evidence, or even by the highest standard of beyond a reasonable doubt, normally reserved for criminal cases? Further, the ATCA does not address the question whether there might be affirmative defenses, or mitigating factors, that a defendant would be entitled to plead in justification or what the proper measure of damages would be in any particular case. Is a recovery to be limited to compensatory damages, or are punitive damages also to be awarded and, if so, at what level? Are compensatory damages to be limited to economic interests?

The court in *Filartiga* suggested that these questions were not jurisdictional but "choice of law" issues, to be resolved later. This was a neat answer but not sufficient when the relevant jurisdictional statute is predicated on the existence of a "tort" in the first instance. In 1789, as today, a tort was more than merely a bad act. It was, and remains, a legally cognizable wrong, for which the law provides a remedy. Although international law, by custom, by treaty, or by both, may well impose certain duties on nation-states (and arguably on individuals in certain limited circumstances), it simply does not provide the balance of the equation; and it did not do so in 1789.

In *Tel-Oren*, Judge Edwards disagreed. He conceded this fundamental difficulty with the court's approach in *Filartiga*, suggesting that it "is consistent with the language of section 1350, [but] places an awesome duty on federal district courts to derive from an amorphous entity—i.e., the 'law of nations'—standards of liability applicable in concrete situations."[54] This, he noted, was not impossible, but he concluded that "the formidable research task involved gives pause, and suggests consideration of a quite plausible alternative construction of section 1350."[55] That alternative was to refer to the domestic tort law of the United States for the necessary cause of action. Leaving aside the obvious question of which U.S. tort law should be applied (there being at least fifty possible models, as well as the District of Columbia, the Commonwealth of Puerto Rico, the Virginia Islands, Guam, or some indeterminate federal version to choose from), Judge Edwards' suggestion of an alternative approach based on a desire to avoid a formidable—and probably impossible—research task reveals most clearly that the ATCA, as interpreted by the Second Circuit in *Filartiga*, is an invitation to the courts to make up the law as they go along.

This probably was not Congress's intention. However, what Congress did intend remains so obscure that it is impossible to say with any certainty. Judge Bork attempted to make sense of the law by suggesting that Congress had in mind the three violations of the law of nations then generally recognized: (1) violation of safe-conducts, (2) infringement of ambassadorial rights, and (3) piracy. This certainly is plausible and, more to the point, was the approach taken by the Supreme Court when it finally did address the ATCA, on the merits, in the spring of 2004.

54. *Id.* at 781.
55. *Id.* at 782.

The "Law of Nations"—Paradigms of 1789

Sosa v. Alvarez-Machain was the latest in a long line of decisions arising out of the 1985 torture and murder of Enrique Camerena-Salazar.[56] Salazar was a U.S. Drug Enforcement Administration agent who was working in Mexico at the time he was killed. American officials came to believe that Alvarez-Machain, a Mexican physician, had participated in Salazar's torture—specifically by keeping the man alive during his "interrogation." Alvarez-Machain was indicted and, after efforts to secure his extradition from Mexico failed, U.S. officials hired several Mexican nationals (including Mr. José Sosa) to seize Alvarez-Machain and bring him to the United States. This led to the Supreme Court's ruling in *United States v. Alvarez-Machain*,[57] in which it decided that the federal courts could exercise jurisdiction over a defendant in these circumstances, even if he had been brought to the United States by "forcible abduction."

In the trial, Alvarez-Machain was acquitted. In 1993 he brought civil actions against the United States, under the Federal Tort Claims Act (FTCA),[58] and against the persons who seized him in Mexico (including Sosa), under the ATCA. The Supreme Court dismissed both claims, concluding that the FTCA's waiver of sovereign immunity did not apply in these circumstances, and that the ATCA was far too narrow in scope to support the action against Sosa.

In addressing the ATCA, the Court recognized that—on its face—the statute was merely jurisdictional. Nevertheless, it also concluded that "at the time of enactment the jurisdiction enabled federal courts to hear claims in a very limited category defined by

56. 124 S. Ct. 2739.
57. 504 U.S. 655 (1992).
58. 28 U.S.C. sec. 1346(b)(1), secs. 2671–2680.

the law of nations and recognized at common law."[59] As Judge Bork had suggested in his *Tel-Oren* opinion twenty years before, the Court concluded that there were only three such claims:

> We think it is correct, then, to assume that the First Congress understood that the district courts would recognize private causes of action for certain torts in violation of the law of nations, though we have found no basis to suspect Congress had any examples in mind beyond those torts corresponding to Blackstone's three primary offenses: violation of safe conducts, infringement of the rights of ambassadors, and piracy.[60]

The Court conceded that it was possible that new torts, cognizable under the ATCA, could develop over time but cautioned that "[w]e think courts should require any claim based on the present-day law of nations to rest on a norm of international character accepted by the civilized world and defined with a specificity comparable to the features of the 18th-century paradigms we have recognized."[61] It was this requirement that the Court held to be "fatal to Alvarez's claim."[62] Although there are a number of international instruments, such as the United Nations Universal Declaration of Human Rights and the International Covenant on Civil and Political Rights, that recognize a right against arbitrary arrest or detention, the Court concluded that neither document imposed binding legal obligations that were "self-executing," that is, enforceable in court without further congressional action. Further, although there was some evidence of a generalized consensus among states against arbitrary detention, this was insufficient to establish a binding norm of customary international law.[63] Alvarez-Machain's ACTA claim was, therefore, dismissed.

59. 124 S. Ct. at 2754.
60. *Id.* at 2761.
61. *Id.* at 2761–2762.
62. *Id.* at 2762.
63. *Id.* at 2769.

This aspect of the Court's ruling met instant criticism—first in Justice Antonin Scalia's opinion (joined by Justice Clarence Thomas and Chief Justice William Rehnquist), concurring in part and in the judgment. Scalia noted that the Court's formulation, that no development since the ACTA was enacted in 1789 had "'categorically *precluded* federal courts from recognizing a claim under the law of nations as an element of common law,'" effectively turned the established rule regarding federal common law "on its head."[64] Since *Erie R. Co. v. Tompkins*, 304 U.S. 64 (1938), he noted, federal courts cannot create "federal common law" without some affirmative congressional authorization. "In holding open the possibility that judges may create rights when Congress has not authorized them to do so, the Court countenances judicial occupation of a domain that belongs to the people's representatives."[65]

The Court's suggestion in *Sosa*, that new causes of action cognizable under the ATCA may develop as the law of nations develops, opened a door that should have been left closed. This is true even though, assuming the lower federal courts will heed the Supreme Court's clear directions that no claims be recognized that enjoy "less definite content and acceptance among civilized nations than the historical paradigms familiar when [the ATCA] was enacted," the opportunities for judicial mischief should be comparatively limited. Widespread state practice demanding respect for safe conducts and diplomatic personnel did exist in 1789, and piracy was widely assumed to be a "universal" offense, even if there was little practice supporting a right to both prescribe *and* prosecute that offense on the international level. Because of the lack of widespread and consistent state practice supporting even core portions of contemporary human rights law, and the inherently controversial nature of binding norms that regulate a state's rela-

64. *Id.* at 2772 (Scalia, J., concurring in part and in the judgment).
65. *Id.* at 2774.

tionship to its own citizens, it is unlikely that more modern norms will achieve the status of these three in the near future. Indeed, in *Sosa v. Alvarez-Machain*, the Supreme Court took an appropriately skeptical approach to such claims.

Nevertheless, the Court has inserted the judiciary into an area uniquely reserved to the political branches, and particularly to the president. Although circumstances arise when the courts are properly called on to interpret or apply treaties to which the United States is party,[66] on the international level it is the president who must construe the United States' legal obligations—whether in treaties or customary international law. He is, as John Marshall noted while serving in the House of Representatives:

> [T]he sole organ of the nation in its external relations, and its sole representative with foreign nations. Of consequence, the demand of a foreign nation can only be made on him. He possesses the whole Executive power. He holds and directs the force of the nation. Of consequence, any act to be performed by the force of the nation is to be performed through him.[67]

The power to interpret American international law obligations is a critical authority. Nation-states often disagree over the content and meaning of international law, whether in treaties or custom, and the view of one state (or grouping of states) is inherently no better or worse than that of others. The right of every state to interpret and apply international law for itself is an essential attribute of sovereignty and, although that right may be subordinated by consent, as when a state has agreed to accept the ruling of an

---

66. *See, e.g., Day v. Trans World Airlines, Inc.,* 528 F.2d 31, 33 (2d Cir. 1975), cert. denied, 429 U.S. 890 (1976) (interpreting provisions of the "Warsaw Convention" dealing with air transport). And, as Justice Scalia pointed out in his *Sosa* opinion, it is the prerogative of Congress and the president to create and define any private causes of action that may arise from treaties to which the United States is a party. Slip op., *supra* note 64, at 11–12.

67. 10 Annals of Congress 596, 613–614 (1800).

international arbitral body like the ICJ, it cannot be extinguished. When American courts recognize and vindicate claims based on an interpretation of international law that is inconsistent with the executive branch's position, they both trench on the president's constitutional authority and undercut the United States' ability to "speak with one voice" in foreign affairs.

In the process, they may very possibly put the United States in an impossible position relative to other powers. Although, all things being equal, the Court's cautious language about the possibility that new ATCA claims can develop may well lessen the potential for interbranch conflicts over the meaning and content of international law, it does not rule them out. It is also important to recall that assertions of jurisdiction by the United States over events overseas can no more make international law, in and of themselves, than can Belgium's ill-starred foray as an international prosecutor. However, the potential damage to the foreign relations of the United States, and to the operation of the international system itself, by such assertions remains substantial.

The Future

Although those who claim that universal jurisdiction is an established fact are asserting far more than they can prove based on the actual practice of states, doubtless a determined effort is under way to create such authority. As noted above, the appeal of "universality" to international activists is obvious, as is its attraction for states who wish to increase their stature in a world where the ability to project military power is increasingly beyond their material means. Moreover, as this effort to substitute what foreign policy wonks call "soft" power for military might is dressed in the language of reason and law—the creation of an international system governed by law and not by force—dissension begins to sound positively seditious.

Basing such a system on universal jurisdiction principles, however, is a short route not to the elysian fields but to international anarchy. Universality presupposes the right of a single state to act on behalf of all in punishing conduct that all consider criminal, regardless of the citizenship or official capacity of the victims and perpetrators. Even if there were agreement among all nations on what conduct that might be (and there is not), the interpretation of even the most well-established international norms differs from state to state. Take, for example, the United Nations Convention on the Prevention and Punishment of the Crime of Genocide. This widely accepted treaty defines genocide to include "[c]ausing serious bodily or mental harm to members of [a protected] group." In ratifying this convention, the United States noted an understanding to the effect that "the term 'mental harm' . . . means permanent impairment of mental faculties through drugs, torture or similar techniques."[68] It was the only state to note such a limitation. Similarly, the United States also noted a reservation providing that "nothing in the Convention requires or authorizes legislation or other action by the United States of America prohibited by the Constitution of the United States as interpreted by the United States."[69] Other states may interpret the convention more broadly (to include causing anguish or depression, for instance) and, in fact, the U.S. reservation on authorizing legislation prohibited by its Constitution was questioned or rejected by as many as thirteen other state-parties. These included Germany, the United Kingdom, Spain, Sweden, Norway, the Netherlands, Mexico, Italy, Ireland, Greece, Finland, Estonia, and Denmark.[70] Under universal jurisdiction theories, these differing views could be imposed on the

68. *See* Declarations and Reservations to the Convention on the Prevention and Punishment of the Crime of Genocide, at U.N. High Commissioner for Human Rights, http://www.unhchr.ch/html/menu3/b/treaty1gen.htm.
69. *Id.*
70. *Id.*

United States, despite its objections, through prosecutions against American citizens or officials.

Similarly, although it is widely accepted that the laws of war prohibit indiscriminate attacks that result in disproportionate damage to civilians, there is wide disagreement over what constitutes such an attack. This issue is raised nearly anytime the United States chooses to use force overseas. It was raised during the 1990–1991 Persian Gulf War, the 1999 NATO campaign against Slobodan Milosevic's Serbia, and, most recently, in Afghanistan and Iraq. Although the United States follows the traditional formulation, that collateral damage to civilians cannot be disproportionate to the military advantage sought to be gained, many of its allies have accepted an arguably far more restrictive standard, based on the 1977 Protocol I Additional to the 1949 Geneva Conventions. The United States has refused to become a party to that protocol.

In fact, under the doctrine of universal jurisdiction, each and every state would be perfectly entitled to interpret the requirements of international law in accord with its own values, traditions, and national interests and then to impose that interpretation on any other state through the device of a criminal prosecution. Thus, for example, if Saddam Hussein's Iraq (or Libya, or China, or the Principality of Monaco) had concluded that the United States and its NATO allies had violated the laws of war by attacking (over the issue of Kosovo) the Federal Republic of Yugoslavia in 1999, it would have been perfectly entitled to indict President Clinton, Secretary of State Madeleine Albright, General Wesley Clark, and any other potentially responsible official, as well as their counterparts in NATO's other member states, and demand their extradition for trial in Baghdad. The Allies would have had no choice but to comply. That, of course, is not the law, and this is precisely and exactly why it is not. Universality cannot work in a system of independent and equal states, in which all may interpret and enforce the law with equal authority—unless it is limited to stateless persons, as pirates once were considered to be.

The International Criminal Court

The lack of such a universal imperium, in which states are subordinate to an international judicial authority, has not stopped determined efforts to create a new international criminal judicial system, based on principles of universality. A little over four months after the ICJ held Belgium's universal jurisdiction experiment to violate international law, the first permanent international criminal court was established (July 1, 2002) at The Hague. Unlike the two United Nations' ad hoc criminal tribunals, for the former Yugoslavia and Rwanda, which have a limited territorial and temporal jurisdiction based ultimately on state consent (under the U.N. Charter all members agree to carry out Security Council resolutions adopted, as these were, under Chapter VII), the ICC asserts a worldwide jurisdiction.[71]

Created in accord with the 1998 Rome Statute, under which the court was not actually established until sixty countries had deposited instruments of ratification, the ICC has competence to investigate, try, and punish dozens of offenses falling into four broad categories: (1) genocide, (2) crimes against humanity, (3) war crimes, and (4) aggression. Under Article 12 of the Statute, the ICC claims the right to exercise this authority with respect to the citizens of state-parties, and of nonstate-parties when an offense has allegedly taken place on the territory of a state-party. This claim violates international law.

Despite its grandiose title of "statute," the ICC's founding doc-

71. Under the United Nations Charter, all member states agree to carry out Security Council resolutions adopted under Chapter VII, "to maintain or restore international peace and security." The Yugoslav and Rwandan tribunals were established under such resolutions in 1993 and 1994, respectively.

ument is nothing more than a treaty. Like all other treaties, it cannot regulate the rights and obligations of third-party states unless they have ratified the instrument through their own constitutional processes. The Rome Statute's effort to upset this long-settled rule is one of the fundamental reasons why the United States has rejected the ICC project. It was noted both by President Clinton, who cited this aspect of the Rome Statute in urging President Bush not to submit the treaty for the Senate's consideration, and by the Bush Administration in explaining why the United States was formally rejecting or "de-signing" the Rome Statute: "We believe that in order to be bound by a treaty, a state must be party to that treaty. The ICC asserts jurisdiction over citizens of states that have not ratified the treaty. This threatens US sovereignty."[72]

A New Sovereignty

The United States' participation in the ICC regime, or even acceptance of a "universal" criminal jurisdiction like that asserted by Belgium, would not merely threaten U.S. sovereignty; it would require a revolution in the very conception of "sovereignty," or self-government, as Americans have understood it for the past two and a quarter centuries. When thirteen of Britain's American colonies established a political union and declared their independence in 1776, they claimed the right to "assume among the powers of the earth, the separate and equal station to which the Laws of Nature and of Nature's God entitle them." That claim was vindicated by war and accepted by Great Britain in the 1783 Treaty of Paris. Since that time, all the other "powers of the earth" have accepted American independence. Among the attributes of sovereignty that came along with this separate and equal station was the right to interpret and apply international law, or the "Law of

72. Remarks of Marc Grossman, Under Secretary of State for Political Affairs, to the Center for Strategic and International Studies, Washington, D.C., May 6, 2002.

Nations" as the Republic's founders would have known it, by and through American institutions, established by and accountable to the American people.

Universality, of course, posits that there is some authority higher than the individual nation-state, an authority capable of second-guessing any particular country's conclusions about what international law requires, what conduct it condemns as criminal, and who may have committed violations. No such authority has been recognized, either spiritual or temporal, since the Peace of Westphalia in 1648, when the Holy Roman Emperor effectively surrendered his claims to a universal authority over central Europe. Today, no single state, or collection of states, can legitimately claim such power. This includes modern, multilateral organizations such as the United Nations (whose Charter plainly reaffirms the "principle of the sovereign equality of all its members"), the ICJ (or the "World Court"), and the World Trade Organization. The legal authority of these institutions rests not on some generalized lawmaking power embodied in the "international community" but solely on the consent of states—a consent that could be withdrawn in appropriate circumstances.

As an institution, the ICC is different from these others in quality and kind. As noted above, the court has asserted jurisdiction over the citizens and public officials of all states, with or without consent. The circumstances in which this claim would apply are as follows. If an offense, otherwise subject to the ICC's authority, is alleged to have been committed on the territory of an ICC member state by the citizen of a nonmember, under the Rome Statute the court would be free to investigate, prosecute, try, and punish that person—regardless of his or her citizenship. Moreover, the court also would be able to reach the citizens and officials of nonparty-states in such circumstances, who may have never set foot in the territory of a member state, on theories of intended consequences and command responsibility. This goes far beyond any territorial or extraterritorial jurisdiction recognized by modern international law. It ignores a number of fundamental limits that international law has traditionally imposed on the ability of one state to prosecute the citizens and officials of another, limits that apply even to prosecutions for offenses committed on a state's own territory.[73]

The ICC's pretensions in this respect are entirely unprecedented, because they involve a kind of criminal enforcement power never before claimed, or conceded, by the community of nations. Unlike traditional "universal" jurisdiction claims, which involve individual states enforcing international norms through national judicial authority, the ICC wields a supernational authority that is exercised in contravention of ordinary state power. Under the doctrine of "complementarity" set forth in Article 17 of the Rome Statute, the court can generally take a case only if national institutions fail to pursue the matter in an impartial manner.[74] The court, of course, is the sole judge (under Rome Statute Article 119) of whether this standard is met. Therefore, in most circumstances, when the ICC goes forward with a case, it will do so in contravention of decisions already made by competent national authorities. The ICC is not, in short, the agent of its member states; it is the principal. This is a fundamentally different kind of international judicial authority than that acknowledged, and exercised, by multilateral institutions in the past.

Not only does this revolutionary institution, as a new species

73. *See* Lee A. Casey and David B. Rivkin Jr., "The Limits of Legitimacy: The Rome Statute's Unlawful Application to Non-State Parties," 44 *Va. J. Int'l L.* 63 (2003).

74. In this regard, Article 17 provides that the ICC must consider a case "inadmissible" in the court unless the state with jurisdiction over the matter is "unwilling or unable genuinely to carry out the investigation or prosecution." Rome Statute of the International Criminal Court, art. 17 (July 17, 1998), at United Nations, http://www.un.org/law/icc/statute/romefra.htm. Cases can also be referred to the court by a state, or by the U.N. Security Council.

of judicial authority, challenge traditional notions of sovereignty and self-government, it also constitutes a new and dangerous form of executive or prosecutorial power. The ICC, of course, does not merely act as a court. Its judicial bench is only one of the ICC's organs. The others are the registrar—who handles administrative matters—and the prosecutor. The power of the ICC prosecutor is enormous and, for all practical purposes, unchecked. Under the Rome Statute, prosecutors may initiate investigations on their own authority, and the court's judges must permit an investigation to proceed if it has a "reasonable basis." Although a prosecutor may be removed from office for "serious misconduct or a serious breach of his or her duties,"[75] these terms have been defined in relation to personal misconduct or attempting to obstruct the course of justice.[76] How he exercises his office, his agenda, is entirely up to the prosecutor.

Powerful prosecutors, of course, are nothing new. As Justice Robert Jackson (then serving as U.S. Attorney General) explained about federal prosecutors:

> The prosecutor has more control over life, liberty, and reputation than any other person in America. His discretion is tremendous. He can have citizens investigated and, if he is that kind of person, he can have this done to the tune of public statements and veiled or unveiled intimations. Or the prosecutor may choose a more subtle course and simply have a citizen's friends interviewed. The prosecutor can order arrests, present cases to the grand jury in secret session, and on the basis of his one-sided presentation of the facts, can cause the citizen to be indicted and held for trial. He may dismiss the cases before trial, in which case the defense never has a chance to be heard. Or he may go on with a public trial. If he obtains a conviction, the prosecutor can still make recommendations as to sentence, as to whether the prisoner should get probation or a suspended sentence, and after he is put

75. Rome Statute of the International Criminal Court, art. 46.
76. Rules of Procedure and Evidence, Rule 24.

away, as to whether he is a fit subject for parole. While the prosecutor at his best is one of the most beneficent forces in our society, when he acts from malice or other base motives, he is one of the worst.[77]

In the United States, however, this power is tempered by democratic accountability. State prosecutors are generally elected officials—often the most important local elected officials. United States Attorneys are appointed by the president, but only by and with the Senate's advice and consent. As Jackson further explained:

> Because of this immense power to strike at citizens, not with mere individual strength, but with all the force of government itself, the post of Federal District Attorney from the very beginning has been safeguarded by presidential appointment, requiring confirmation of the Senate of the United States. You are thus required to win an expression of confidence in your character by both the legislative and the executive branches of the government before assuming the responsibilities of a federal prosecutor.[78]

Moreover, in actual practice, the enforcement policies and decisions of individual United States Attorneys are subject to the president's direction and to oversight by Congress.

Perhaps more to the point, even assuming that a prosecutor is acting from good and honorable motives, he exercises some of the most fundamental powers of government—and this must be accomplished in the context of his or her own body politic. The essence of prosecutorial discretion is balancing the necessity of punishing an individual against broader societal interests. At one level, it entails examining the accused's genuine culpability—whether the alleged violation was willful and deliberate, whether the person involved was a repeat offender, and how serious the offense was

77. Robert H. Jackson, *The Federal Prosecutor*, "Speech to Second Annual Conference of United States Attorneys," Apr. 1, 1940, at http://www.roberthjackson.org/theman2-7-6-1.asp.

78. *Id.*

compared with other offenses that might merit expending prosecutorial resources. The answers to these questions are often highly localized, and this is particularly true of resource allocation questions. One area may have significant problems with street crime, while another may be plagued by organized crime, and still another by a corrupt local political system. In exercising his discretion, a democratically accountable prosecutor must address the needs of the community he serves. From this grows legitimacy.

International prosecutors, of course, do not serve any particular community to which they are accountable. They suffer a corresponding lack of very basic legitimacy. The ICC prosecutor's detachment from the polities over which he exercises authority exacerbates another of the potential abuses of prosecutorial power highlighted by Jackson. In choosing his or her cases, a prosecutor can also choose his or her defendants: "Therein is the most dangerous power of the prosecutor; that he will pick people that he thinks he should get, rather than pick cases that need to be prosecuted."[79] This danger is real enough in the national or domestic context but is at least checked by the systemic limitations on a prosecutor's authority. In the end, he must live in the community where he operates and where he can expect that another will one day exercise his power. The ICC prosecutor may be, almost certainly will be, entirely detached from the countries and localities where he exercises his authority. For example, the current ICC prosecutor is a citizen of Argentina. His first investigations, however, will involve actions in Africa, specifically in Uganda and the Democratic Republic of the Congo. Both states have actually requested the prosecutor's intervention, evidently having concluded that they are unable to handle the cases themselves.[80] Nevertheless,

79. *Id.*
80. *See* "President of Uganda refers situation concerning the Lord's Resistance Army (LRA) to the ICC" (Jan. 29, 2004), at International Criminal Court, http://www.icc-cpi.int/newspoint/articles/29.html; "Prosecutor receives referral of the situ-

in investigating and prosecuting persons in these countries, the prosecutor will bring with him his own national and professional perspectives and assumptions, which may or may not have much in common with those of the accused or of their alleged victims.

It must be emphasized, of course, that the potential for abuse here does not depend on the ICC prosecutor's acting in bad faith; far from it. America's own experience, in the 1980s and 1990s, with the now justly discredited Independent Counsel Statute establishes beyond doubt that a prosecutorial authority that has deliberately been separated from the normal institutions of national justice, and that exercises jurisdiction over a particular category of people—can lead to abuses—regardless of how dedicated and honorable individual prosecutors may be. This comparison is not far-fetched if we consider that prosecutors of the U.N. tribunals have seen their raison d'être as the prosecution of senior government officials of sovereign states who, in their view, have committed serious violations of international law and gotten away with it.[81] There is little reason to expect that the ICC prosecutor will see his mission differently.

A European Project

Because of these very troubling aspects of the ICC as an institution, the United States has not ratified the Rome Statute and is not likely

---

ation in the Democratic Republic of Congo" (Apr. 19, 2004), at International Criminal Court, http://www.icc-cip.int/newspoint/pressreleases/19.html.

81. Canadian Justice Louise Arbour, during her tenure as prosecutor for both the ad hoc U.N. international criminal tribunals, the International Criminal Tribunal for the Former Yugoslavia, and the International Criminal Tribunal for Rwanda, viewed her role as, at least in part, teaching the relevant populations that they had chosen the wrong leaders through democratic processes: " It's important to permit these people to recognize that they made a very serious error in judgment. In electing these people, they have to let go of them as national heroic figures." Frontline, "The World's Most Wanted Man," interview with Louise Arbour, at http://www. pbs.org/wgbh/pages/frontline/shows/karadzic/interviews/arbour.html.

to become a state-party in the foreseeable future. Although the United States was involved in the original negotiations leading up to the ICC's creation (seeking all along some effective means of limiting the court's power), today the ICC's primary backers are the states of the European Union (EU). The EU's twenty-five members represent the largest voting bloc in the Rome Statute's Assembly of States Parties, and eight of the ICC's eighteen judges are from EU countries. Perhaps not surprisingly, the EU has made ICC "universality" a priority.[82]

   To that end, it has embarked on a worldwide political campaign with the "crucial objective with regard to third States [being] to maximize the political will for the ratification and implementation of the Statute to achieve the desired universality."[83] Among other things, the EU has funded pro-ICC groups in the United States, such as the Coalition for the International Criminal Court, seeking to influence American policy. In addition, it has vigorously opposed the United States' efforts to obtain a series of "Article 98" agreements, which are designed to protect American citizens from the ICC's reach unless the Rome Statute is ratified in accord with our own constitutional processes. The EU has also made ICC membership a requirement for new EU member states—going so far as to rebuke Romania, when it was an EU aspirant, for entering an Article 98 agreement with the United States.[84]

82. *See, e.g.*, "EU Statement on the Inauguration of the International Criminal Court" (Mar. 13, 2003), at European Union, http://europa.eu.int/comm/external_relations/osce/stment/icc120303.htm. Ironically, of course, the very fact that ICC state parties established the court's jurisdiction through a treaty is itself an acknowledgment that no such authority exists separate and apart from the consent of individual states. It cannot be universal in character until it has been accepted by all.

83. "EU Action Plan to Follow-up on the Common Position on the International Criminal Court" (May 15, 2002), at European Union, http://europa.eu.int/comm/external_relations/human_rights/doc/icc05_02.htm.

84. *See* "U.S. Military Aid Tied to Court Immunity" (Aug 14, 2002), at Cable News Network, http://www.cnn.com/2002/ALLPOLITICS /08/14/aid.criminalcourts/.

Regrettably, many of the ICC's proponents, including the states of the EU who know better, claim that the United States is somehow seeking "impunity" under international law by its efforts to protect its citizens from the ICC's unwarranted and illegal claims.[85] Such statements, which suggest that the United States is somehow inherently subject to the ICC's authority and is attempting to repudiate legally binding obligations, reveal either a cynical strategy to mislead the general public or an appalling ignorance of the actual record of universal jurisdiction as an international law doctrine— perhaps both. Far from the United States' seeking immunity, or impunity, under international law, its position on the ICC's jurisdictional claims is far better grounded than that of its opponents.

For states, such as the members of the EU, who already have accepted the subordination of their national institutions and interests to a supernational body, an ICC jurisdiction that can be applied on a uniform and efficient basis may well be acceptable. For the United States, however, whose national existence is justified only by a long-ago claim to the right of self-government, "laying its foundation on such principles and organizing its powers in such form, as to them shall seem most likely to effect their Safety and Happiness,"[86] the acceptance of such a supernational authority would be revolutionary.

It would require the American people to accept that they no longer hold the ultimate authority over their own destiny but that they and their elected representatives must answer to a foreign power over which they have no control and precious little influence. It may be that in the future, a time will come when the

---

85. *See, e.g.,* "Human Rights Watch, EU Commitment to Criminal Court Facing Test" (Aug. 28, 2002) at Human Rights Watch, http://www.hrw.org/press/2002/08/article98-0828.htm.

86. Declaration of Independence, par. 2.

peoples of the world do share the same values, interests, and concepts of justice and due process, to an extent that America's claim to self-government will become superfluous. Judging by present circumstances, however, that day has not yet dawned—and it promises to be a long time in coming.

Index

188